ESSAYS IN INTERNATIONAL FINANCE

No. 172, May 1989

ACCOUNTING FOR LOSSES ON SOVEREIGN DEBT: IMPLICATIONS FOR NEW LENDING

JACK M. GUTTENTAG

AND

RICHARD HERRING

INTERNATIONAL FINANCE SECTION

DEPARTMENT OF ECONOMICS
PRINCETON UNIVERSITY
PRINCETON, NEW JERSEY

Library of Congress Cataloging-in-Publication Data

Guttentag, Jack M., 1923-
  Accounting for losses on sovereign debt.

  (Essays in international finance, ISSN 0071-142X ;   no. 172 (May 1989)
  Bibliography: p.
  1. Loans, Foreign—Accounting.   2. Banks and banking, International—
Accounting.   3. Loans, Foreign—Developing countries.   I. Herring,
Richard.   II. Title.   III. Series: Essays in international finance   ;   no. 172.
HG136.P7   no.   172 [HG3891.5]   332'.042 s   88-34742
ISBN 0-88165-079-X   [332.1'5'0681]

Printed in the United States of America by Princeton University Press at Princeton, New Jersey.

International Standard Serial Number: 0071-142X
International Standard Book Number: 0-88165-079-X
Library of Congress Catalog Card Number: 88-34742

CONTENTS

LIST OF TABLES

LIST OF FIGURES

ACCOUNTING FOR LOSSES ON SOVEREIGN DEBT: IMPLICATIONS FOR NEW LENDING

1 Introduction

This essay had its genesis in two observations about the behavior of banks since the Mexican debt crisis in mid-August 1982. First, some banks have accumulated substantial reserves and taken large charge-offs against claims on developing countries (see Table 1). Although often these actions have been taken voluntarily, sometimes they have been responses to mandatory provisioning requirements imposed by regulatory authorities (see Table 2 for a summary of provisioning policies in several key banking centers). Second, most banks have substantially increased accounting measures of their capital-to-assets ratios—in many cases at least partly in response to pressure from regulators (see Table 3). As we show later, market-based measures of capital strength have also improved.

In this essay, we examine the implications of these developments for future bank lending to developing countries. More specifically, we focus on how decisions about provisioning and charge-offs are made and how these decisions (along with the balance-sheet consequences of past accounting decisions) affect new lending decisions.

Since the Mexican debt crisis in 1982, the volume of new lending to developing countries has dropped sharply, as shown in Figure 1. Indeed, in several years the change in claims on *all* non-OPEC developing countries has been less than the flow of concerted lending arranged for countries that adopted adjustment programs supported by the International Monetary Fund (Watson et al., 1988, p. 76). We term such concerted loans "bailout" loans because they are made to countries that are unable to borrow from any lenders to whom they are not already indebted. While the change in the stock of outstanding loans understates the volume of new loans to some extent, the volume of other "spontaneous" loans appears to have been negligible.[1]

The authors are grateful to Santanu Sarkar for research assistance; to Mark Tousey for data; to Andrew Crockett, David Folkerts-Landau, Arminio Fraga, William Hood, Donald Mathieson, and Maxwell Watson for helpful comments on an earlier draft; and to the Ford foundation for financial support.

[1] The change in the stock of outstanding loans is a downwardly biased measure of new lending because it does not account for loan charge-offs, sales to nonbank investors, the exercise of official guarantees, and repayments of principal, including reductions of interest-rate arrearages.

1

TABLE 1

PROVISIONS, RESERVES, AND CHARGE-OFFS AGAINST LDC DEBT, 1987
(*in millions of dollars*)

Selected U.S. Banks	Date Announced	LDC Provisions during		LDC Charge-Offs during 1987	Total Reported LDC Reserves as a % of Total LDC Claims
		1987II	1987IV		
Citicorp	5/19	$3,000	$ 0	$214	25%
Chase Manhattan	5/27	1,600	0	78	25
Bank of Boston	6/3	300	200	200	55 [a]
BankAmerica	6/8	1,100	0	234	20
Chemical NY	6/11	1,100	0	21	25
First Chicago	6/15	780	240	91	39
First Interstate	6/11	500	180	150	54 [a]
Manufacturers Hanover	6/16	1,700	0	63	22
Bankers Trust NY	6/18	700	0	55	25
J. P. Morgan	7/8	850	0	149	25

Estimated Average LDC Reserves as a % of Total LDC Claims
for Major Banks outside the United States

Canada	35% to 40%
Germany	40% or more
Japan	5%
Switzerland	30% or more
United Kingdom	30%

[a] Total reserves are reported as a percentage of all nontrade related claims rather than all claims.

SOURCE: Compiled from data in Hanley et al. (1988a) and McDermott (1987).

The decline in lending is primarily a reflection of fundamental economic forces—slow growth in the world economy, high real interest rates, and domestic, economic, and political problems in the major borrowing countries—factors we treat as exogenous. Any independent influence of provisioning and charge-offs has been secondary. But since public policy can have some influence on provisions and charge-offs, it is useful to ask how these factors affect new lending, given the fundamental economic forces.

TABLE 2

Minimum Loan-Loss Reserves against LDC Exposures Established by Regulatory Authorities in Selected Industrial Countries, Year-End 1987

France	No formal rules, but the banking commission has encouraged banks to establish reserves of at least 30% of developing-country exposure.
Germany	No formal rules, but leading banks have up to 100% coverage.
Japan	The Ministry of Finance requires a 5% reserve, which is also the maximum.
Spain	The Bank of Spain requires a minimum 35% reserve against rescheduling countries.
United Kingdom	In mid-1987, the Bank of England proposed a series of guidelines based on a scoring system for individual countries. The application of this system would require the establishment of reserves of 25 to 30%
United States	The three federal bank-regulatory authorities have imposed Allocated Transfer Risk Reserves against several of the smaller rescheduling countries after judging claims on them to be "value impaired."

SOURCE: For all countries except the United States, Hanley et al. (1988a, p. 37); for the United States, GAO (1988, p. 26). See text for further discussion of U.S. Allocated Transfer Risk Reserve.

To anticipate our conclusions, on the one hand, both the increased provisions and charge-offs on outstanding claims on debtor countries and the increased capital strength of the banks have diminished the willingness of banks to participate in future "bailout" loans. On the other hand, increased capital strength will ultimately facilitate a resumption of spontaneous lending to countries that have demonstrated an ability to resume servicing their debt.

Section 2 reviews the basic accounting principles that guide decisions to set aside provisions and make charge-offs and contrasts these principles with bank practice. Section 3 examines accounting and economic measures of a bank's capacity to bear loss and considers the conditions under which one or the other is relevant to the bank's lending decision. Sections 4 and 5 examine the bank decision process with regard to bailout loans and considers how it may be influenced by past provisions and charge-offs and by changes in the capacity to bear loss. This analysis, which is based on the formal model developed in the Appendix, assumes first that only economic values matter to the bank in its lending decisions. It then considers the case where accounting consequences also matter. Section 6 broadens the analysis by showing how provisioning and charge-offs can make it more difficult to achieve collective

3

TABLE 3

TRENDS IN CAPITAL-ASSET RATIOS OF BANKS IN
SELECTED INDUSTRIAL COUNTRIES
(*in percent*)

	1982	1983	1984	1985	1986
Canada	3.7	4.1	4.4	4.6	5.0
France	2.1	2.0	1.9	2.2	2.6
Germany	3.3	3.3	3.4	3.5	3.6
Japan	5.0	5.2	5.2	4.8	4.8
Luxembourg	3.5	3.6	3.8	4.0	4.1
Netherlands	4.6	4.7	4.8	5.0	5.2
Switzerland:					
Largest 5 banks	7.3	7.1	7.1	7.8	7.8
All banks	7.5	7.3	7.4	7.9	7.9
United Kingdom:					
Largest 4 banks	7.5	7.3	7.4	7.8	7.9
All banks	4.1	4.4	4.5	5.5	5.4
United States:					
9 money center banks	4.9	5.4	6.2	6.8	7.3
Next 15 banks	5.3	5.7	6.6	7.2	7.5
All country reporting banks	5.6	5.9	6.5	6.9	7.2

SOURCE: Watson et al. (1988, p. 39). Because countries differ markedly in accounting conventions and definitions of capital, these ratios cannot be meaningfully compared across countries, but they do reflect trends within each country.

action on bailout loans that are to be parceled out among the many banks that share claims against country borrowers. Section 7 shows how provisioning can reduce the willingness of banks to resume spontaneous lending to countries in good standing. Section 8 considers Citicorp's dramatic decision in mid-1987 to make a special $3 billion provision against its claims on troubled debtor countries and asks what this might presage for the future of both bailout and spontaneous lending.

2 Provisions, Reserves, and Charge-Offs: Theory and Practice

Balance-Sheet Mechanics

Banks in the United States are expected to recognize and anticipate credit losses through a quarterly charge against earnings known as the "provision for loan loss"—or, for short, "provisions." (The process of deducting a pro-

FIGURE 1
BANK LENDING TO DEVELOPING COUNTRIES, 1979-87II

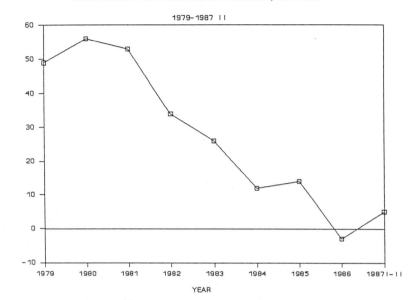

vision from earnings in the current period is termed "provisioning.") This charge is credited to a "loan-loss reserve," which is a contra-asset item on the balance sheet.[2] When a particular asset is deemed to be uncollectable, the amount of the loss is deducted from the loan-loss reserve and thus does not affect current income. The deduction is termed a "charge-off."

Tables 4 and 5 show standard formats for reporting bank income and balance-sheet data. The provision for loan losses (item 3 in Table 4) is an addition to the loan-loss reserve (items 2 and 15 in Table 5). The reserve is reduced by the amount of any charge-offs during the current period (item 13 in Table 5) and increased by the amount of any recoveries in connection with credits that were charged off in prior periods (item 12 in Table 5).

If provisions exceed net income during the period, the remaining deficiency is charged to retained earnings. This is what happened when Citibank added $3 billion to its loan-loss reserve in the second quarter of 1987. When added to the $403 million provision for possible credit losses in the rest of the bank's portfolio, the total provision amounted to $3.403 billion, exceed-

---

[2] The federal regulatory agencies include the provision for loan losses and the loan-loss reserve in the Consolidated Reports of Condition and Income (Call Reports) that all federally insured banks are required to file quarterly. The SEC imposes similar requirements on bank holding companies.

5

TABLE 4

1. Interest Income

2. Less: Interest Expense

3. Less: Provision for Loan Losses

5. Plus: Noninterest Income

6. Plus: Gains (Losses) on Securities Not Held in Trading Accounts

7. Less: Noninterest Expense

8. Less: Applicable Income Taxes

9. Plus: Extraordinary Items and Other Adjustments Net of Income Taxes

10. Equals: Net Income (Loss)

11. Less: Dividends Declared

12. Equals: Addition to (Subtraction from) Retained Earnings

ing income during the quarter by $2.585 billion (see Table 6). This was the largest loss ever reported by a commercial bank during any quarter and, when added to the $117 million dividend that Citibank declared, resulted in a $2.702 billion reduction in retained earnings (Citicorp, 1987).[3] We discuss the reasons for this dramatic accounting event, as well as its potential consequences, in section 7.

In some countries, provisions may be identified with specific assets or categories of assets. The resulting reserve (which may be a liability or a contra-asset account) is termed a "specific" or "allocated" reserve. The distinction between a specific provision and a general provision (or between allocated and unallocated reserves) is of importance chiefly because some regulatory authorities (including the U.S. authorities) regard unallocated reserves, but not allocated reserves, as capital for purposes of meeting capital requirements.

Accounting Principles

In principle, the unallocated loan-loss reserve is the value of anticipated future charge-offs on the existing loan portfolio that cannot yet be identified with any particular asset. As soon as a loss can be identified with a particular asset, a reserve is supposed to be allocated to that asset or the asset is supposed to be charged off, leaving the remainder of the reserve as a buffer against *potential* future losses.

---

[3] A positive adjustment for foreign-currency translation reduced the impact of the deficit on net income on retained earnings by $6 million.

6

TABLE 5

STANDARD BALANCE-SHEET FORMAT

Assets
1. Assets
2. Less: Loan-Loss Reserve
3. Equals: Net Assets

Liabilities
4. Deposits
5. Plus: Other Liabilities
6. Equals: Total Liabilities

Equity Capital
7. Common and Perpetual Preferred stock
8. Plus: Capital Surplus
9. Plus: Retained Earnings
10. Equals: Total Equity Capital
   Net Assets (3) − Total Liabilities (6) = Total Equity Capital (10)

Memorandum item: Loan-Loss Reserve
11. Loan-Loss Reserve Balance at End of Previous Reporting Period
12. Plus: Recoveries
13. Less: Charge-Offs
14. Plus: Provision for loan losses (item 3 in Table 4)
15. Equals: Loan-Loss Reserve (2)

Memorandum item: Retained Earnings
16. Retained Earnings at End of Previous Reporting Period
17. Plus: Net Income (item 10 from Table 4)
18. Less: Cash Dividends Declared (item 11 from Table 4)
19. Plus: Foreign-Currency Translation
20. Equals: Retained Earnings (9)

TABLE 6

IMPACT OF PROVISIONING ON CITICORP'S INCOME STATEMENT
(in billions of dollars)

Net Income before Provision for Loan Losses	$0.818
Less: Provisions for Loan Losses [3]	3.403
Equals: Net Income (Loss) [10]	(2.585)
Less: Dividends Declared [11]	(0.117)
Equals: Addition to (Subtraction from) Retained Earnings [12]	(2.702)

NOTE: Numbers in brackets refer to items in Table 4.

7

It is analytically convenient to view the provision for loan losses as having two components. The first component is a default premium that is established when each loan is extended and is collected as part of the interest payment in each period. The second component is an adjustment for any positive or negative change in economic conditions that affects the prospects for loss on the loan portfolio.

In principle, the bank determines provisions in each period by evaluating the adequacy of the existing loan-loss reserve for each major category of loan. Such judgments take into account any changes in the reserve that may have occurred over the reporting period, reflected in recoveries net of charge-offs (item 12 less item 13 in Table 5). Given the existing reserve, the relevant question is how much larger the reserve should be to absorb additional anticipated losses due to changes in the size or composition of the loan portfolio during the period, as well as to changes in the economic outlook that will affect future losses. The gap between the loan-loss reserve that management now considers appropriate and the existing reserve is the provision that should be allocated from current income.

Since the adequacy of the loss reserve can be drastically affected by perceived changes in the economic outlook, the gap between the existing reserve and the reserve considered adequate may occasionally become very large—far larger than could be covered by an allocation from income during the period. But an exceptionally large provision need not imply that management's view of the economic outlook has deteriorated sharply. Accounting practice often diverges markedly from accounting principles.

Accounting Practice

Bank managers can exercise substantial discretion regarding the timing of provisions because judgments regarding potential future losses are inherently subjective. This is particularly true in the case of sovereign debt, where repayment depends heavily on political will in addition to financial capacity. Furthermore, a definitive loss on loans to (or guaranteed by) sovereign governments occurs only when a loan is repudiated, restructured on a concessionary basis, or sold below book value. Barring such a definitive event, there is always a chance, however slight, that the claim will be collected. Although charge-offs often have a more objective basis—for example, when a borrower terminates operations and is liquidated—even seemingly hopeless situations are sometimes favorably resolved. (That is why one component of the loan-loss reserve, item 12 in Table 5, is "recoveries" of amounts previously charged off.)

So long as investors and regulators rely heavily on financial statements to evaluate a bank, the bank's managers will have an understandable aversion to reporting a decline in net income and equity capital. Larger provisions reduce net income (and compensation tied to net income) and may cause the regulatory authorities to curtail the bank's discretion to pay dividends.[4] Moreover, charge-offs that exceed provisions reduce the stated (though not necessarily the real) capacity of the bank to bear future losses. Indeed, the bank's solvency may be in question if the amounts involved are large enough. Thus it is not surprising that managers often exercise their discretion to take smaller provisions and charge-offs than might seem warranted to outsiders.

Constraints on Bank Discretion

Although bank provisioning and charge-off decisions are, in the first instance, the prerogative of a bank's management, they are subject to review by several external groups that are likely to take a less optimistic view of the bank's loan portfolio. The first such group is the bank's own external auditors. If the auditors believe the bank's provisions or charge-offs are insufficient, they can insist that the bank increase them or can insert a qualification in their certification of the accuracy and completeness of the bank's financial statements. In taking this stance, the auditors risk being fired. But if they defer to the optimistic view of the bank's managers and it is not borne out by subsequent events, the bank's shareholders may sue the auditors for misrepresenting the financial condition of the bank. Moreover, if the bank's condition deteriorates to the point that it requires an injection of funds from the Federal Deposit Insurance Corporation, the auditors may be sued for having failed to warn the bank's managers about the deterioration of the bank's condition.[5]

Provisions and loan-loss reserves by major banks are also carefully monitored by bank security analysts, who advise investors regarding the relative attractiveness of bank stocks and the relative safety of uninsured claims on banks. The loan-loss provision divided by net charge-offs is considered a key indicator of credit quality. Since a bank's loan portfolio normally grows, the presumption is that this ratio will exceed 1. If it does not, the bank will usually be obliged to explain why its net charge-offs were abnormally large in the current period or why it believes that its exposure to credit risk has diminished. Similarly, a bank with a relatively low ratio of loan-loss reserves to total loans may be obliged to explain why its reserves are not deficient. (The bank usually attempts to make a case that its lending standards are more

---

[4] Continental Illinois National Bank is a striking example of a bank that avoided making adequate provisions in order to continue paying its customary dividend. A bank supervisor in another Western country told us that when he asked a major bank to defend its current provisions, the bank presented an algorithm that, on close examination, made provisions a residual *after* payment of the *customary* dividend.

[5] In the wake of the collapse of Continental Illinois National Bank, the FDIC unsuccessfully sued Ernst & Whinney, the auditors of Continental Illinois, for having failed to warn senior bank officers about the shaky condition of loans purchased from Penn Square (Bailey, 1987, p. 6).

conservative than those of its peers or that it charges off weak loans more aggressively.)

The provisioning decision is subject to further review by the regulatory authorities. In the United States, the Securities and Exchange Commission monitors provisions for loan-loss reserves to make sure that income is reported accurately to investors. If the SEC finds the provision to be inadequate, it may force the bank to publish revised financial statements, amend its procedures for determining provisions, or face a penalty.[6]

The bank supervisory authorities in the United States also monitor the adequacy of a bank's loan-loss reserves and charge-offs as part of their evaluation of a bank's capital adequacy and the enforcement of capital requirements. Indeed, the classification of bank loans is a fundamental part of the examination process. Bank examiners classify loans of questionable quality as "substandard," "doubtful," or "loss." Loans classified as "loss" are deducted from capital, while partial deductions may be made for loans falling into the other classifications.[7] In addition, as a routine part of every examination, bank examiners discuss with a bank's managers the need for additional charge-offs and review the record of charge-offs since the last examination (GAO, 1988, p. 64).

Since February 1984, U.S. banks have been required to maintain a specific loan-loss reserve against claims on the most seriously troubled sovereign debtors. A provision of the International Lending Supervision Act (*Federal Register*, 49, Feb. 13, 1984, p. 5591) requires that banks establish an Allocated Transfer Risk Reserve (ATRR) when the Interagency Country Exposure Review Committee (ICERC), representing the three federal banking agencies, determines that claims on a particular country are "value impaired." The ATRR is an addition to and separate from the unallocated loan-loss reserve and is not counted as primary capital in evaluating the bank's capital adequacy.[8]

The ICERC is obliged to classify claims on a country as value impaired when a country has not made full interest payments for more than six months, or has not met the terms of its restructuring agreement for over one

[6] In June 1987, First Chicago Corporation, in an agreement with the SEC, restated its 1983 and 1984 financial results and agreed to revise its loan-loss reserve procedures without admitting or denying charges that it had violated the corporate-reporting and internal-control provision of the securities law. First Chicago insisted in 1984 that "a huge batch of loans had all gone sour at once. The SEC contended that the loans went bad over a period of time and that loss provisions should have been taken earlier" (Ingersoll and Bailey, 1987, p. 7).

[7] One approach has been to deduct 50 percent of loans classified "doubtful" and 20 percent of those classified "substandard." An additional category, "other," is used to classify loans that have some deficiency in documentation that the bank is obliged to remedy.

[8] See Guttentag and Herring (1985a, pp. 22-25) for an extended discussion of the ATRR and the context in which it was adopted.

year, or has not complied with its IMF stabilization program and shows no immediate prospect for compliance, or appears unlikely to resume an orderly restoration of debt-service payments in the near future. For countries classified as value impaired, banks are obliged to set aside an ATRR equal to a specified percentage (usually 10 percent) of the face value of the loan or to charge off an equivalent amount of the loan. The ATRR increases each year (usually by an additional 15 percent) so long as the country is classified as value impaired.

The classification criteria provide the agencies with substantial discretion, which they have used to avoid requiring an ATRR against claims on any of the largest debtor countries.[9] Claims on eight of the smaller debtor countries, representing collectively less than 2 percent of U.S. bank claims on developing countries, have been classified as value impaired. Few, if any, banks have established ATRRs, however. This is partly because the prospects for repayment of the relevant claims have been so poor, and the amounts involved so small, that the banks voluntarily charged them off before the ATRR was imposed. Moreover, banks find it less costly to charge off a loan than to establish an ATRR, because a loan is subject to a capital requirement so long as it remains on the balance sheet.

Although the supervisory authorities have generally encouraged banks to increase their loan-loss reserves, IRS regulations have steadily reduced incentives for banks to make loan-loss provisions. Until the mid-1970s, U.S. banks could deduct provisions from taxable income until they had accumulated a tax-deductible loan-loss reserve equal to 2.4 percent of eligible loans (a total that excludes government-guaranteed loans). Beginning in the mid-1970s, this permissible reserve was gradually reduced until it reached six-tenths of 1 percent of eligible loans in the mid-1980s. Under the tax law that became effective in 1987, banks are no longer permitted to deduct provisions from taxable income, only losses as evidenced by charge-offs, sales, or other dispositions of loans. Because the new law increased the U.S. tax liabilities of most major banks, however, they may now obtain larger tax savings from charge-offs than they formerly did from provisions.[10]

In summary, practice often departs from principle in determining provi-

[9] For example, even though Brazil's interest moratorium during 1987 lasted more than six months, the three agencies did not require an ATRR against bank claims on Brazil.

[10] Although the marginal tax rate has declined from 46 or 48 percent to 34 percent, the base on which banks are taxed has expanded substantially. Indeed, under the previous tax law several leading banks paid negligible federal income taxes. Moreover, the new tax law requires that banks repay the Treasury for provisions that were permissible deductions in earlier years. The recapture will take place over four years—10 percent of the tax-deductible loan-loss reserve will be taxable in the first year; 20 percent in the second; 30 percent in the third; and 40 percent in the fourth. The recaptured amount will be taxed at the new lower rate, however, whereas past deductions were taken at higher rates.

11

sions and charge-offs because banks have substantial scope for taking an optimistic view of future loan losses. Although a bank's freedom to underprovision or avoid charge-offs may be limited to some extent by the monitoring efforts of auditors, security analysts, or the supervisory authorities, the values that banks report on their balance sheets—net of loan-loss reserves—frequently overstate the market value of assets.

A preoccupation with provisions and loan-loss reserves, furthermore, can be highly misleading. The underlying concern that prompts so much attention to them is the bank's "capacity to bear loss," the decline in asset values that the bank can absorb without jeopardizing the claims of its depositors and other creditors. The loan-loss reserve is an inadequate measure of a bank's capacity to bear loss. Since that capacity may be an important concern of bank managers in making lending decisions, we now examine the concept in more detail.

3 Accounting Measures and the Capacity to Bear Loss

Alternative Measures of the Capacity to Bear Loss

The fundamental component of a bank's capacity to bear loss is shareholders' equity. Indeed, this is the only component of capital about which all supervisory authorities agree (BIS, 1987). The book value of equity (item 10 in Table 5) is one accounting measure of the capacity to bear loss. The loan-loss reserve (item 2 in Table 5) is often added to form a more comprehensive measure that corresponds closely to the U.S. concept of "primary capital" on which capital requirements are based.[11]

The market value of equity has two major advantages over the book value of equity, with or without loan-loss reserves, as a measure of a bank's capacity to bear loss. First, it overcomes the upward bias in the book value of assets that was noted in the preceding section. Second, it is a much more comprehensive measure, because it reflects not only the items that appear on conventional balance sheets but also the present value of off-balance-sheet items such as the bank's commitments, forward contracts, options, lines of credit, acceptances, and intangible assets like the bank's charter and customer relationships.

At year-end 1987, the ratio of the market value of equity to book value of equity for nine major U.S. banks ranged from 46 to 136 percent. The lower

[11] The relevant measure of the capacity to bear loss for regulatory purposes is not necessarily the same as for bank decision-making. Some (but *not* all) regulators consider subordinated debt or preferred stock to be part of the capacity to bear loss because these items protect depositors or because the bank may be able to continue operations despite failure to make payments on them. Regulators also disagree about whether loan-loss reserves should be included.

figure applied to Bank America and reflected the market's judgment that the bank's assets, including some of its claims on developing countries, were substantially overvalued. Eight of the nine banks had ratios below 100 percent. Only J. P. Morgan had a ratio above 100 percent. Which measure of the capacity to bear loss is relevant for bank lending decisions?

Book-Value Measures and Bank Behavior

Financial economists steeped in the efficient-markets literature are skeptical that book values matter in bank decision-making. Many would argue that equity prices accurately reflect all relevant information about the bank, regardless of the accounting conventions and decisions adopted by the bank. In essence, they argue that since bank managers can't fool the equity markets it is pointless for them to try.

A substantial volume of evidence supports this argument, at least regarding the market for equities of the major U.S. banks that are engaged in cross-border lending. Public disclosure about these banks is extensive, including disclosure of information regarding significant exposures to foreign borrowers. Beebe (1985), Kyle and Sachs (1984), and Sachs and Huizinga (1987) show that some of the divergence between market and book values is attributable to discounts applied to the book values of claims on troubled debtor countries. Others (Schoder and Vankudre, 1986, and Smirlock and Kaufold, 1987) suggest that bank-equity markets revalued bank stocks very quickly following the Mexican debt crisis of August 1982. Furthermore, as we note later, the equity market's positive reaction to Citicorp's 1987 announcement of a record $2.6 billion book-value loss indicates that the market was looking through accounting data to market values.

The argument is less persuasive when applied to some markets outside the United States. In many countries very limited information about banks is disclosed to the public, a practice that is often encouraged and abetted by supervisory authorities. In some countries, banks are urged to disguise fluctuations in income and the market value of assets by making allocations to hidden reserves during good times and drawing from them in bad times (Guttentag and Herring, 1986b). If markets have no information other than what the banks report publicly, banks may be able to use accounting conventions to encourage the equity market to take too optimistic a view of their condition.

Even if equity markets look through book values, markets for uninsured deposits and other claims may not. Bank creditors generally do not invest much time or money in evaluating banks; they tend to classify them as either safe or questionable. Banks fear that a major charge-off or a sharp drop in reported earnings will cause a significant number of creditors, including other banks, to shift the bank into the questionable category, raising its cost of funds and perhaps causing losses from the hurried sale of illiquid assets. Fear of this type of creditor reaction is probably the major reason that bankers often object strongly to supervisory suggestions or orders that they reduce accounting measures of asset values or income.[12]

In the United States, the growing importance of money-market funds as holders of uninsured bank deposits has exacerbated this problem. While the managers of these funds may be quite sophisticated in their evaluation of the soundness of banks, their clients are generally unsophisticated investors who would be alarmed to learn that their fund was holding claims on a bank being portrayed adversely in news reports. As a result, fund managers are among the first to withdraw deposits from a bank that reports unexpectedly low earnings or a reduction in capital. (As we shall see, the managers of Citicorp feared just such a response, but they were able to convince the markets that the record loss they reported was in fact a sign of strength.)

Book values may also matter to banks because they matter to regulators. Capital requirements, for example, are defined in terms of book values. If a bank's capital falls below the regulatory minimum, the bank may be subject to closer surveillance than usual, and it may lose its freedom of action on mergers and acquisitions, dividend payments, branch expansion, advertising expenditures, and even loan policy. Indeed, a serious shortfall in book capital that is not remedied quickly can be cause for merging the bank or replacing the management.

If creditors and regulators do react to changes in book values, the use of book values in the bank's decision-making is not inconsistent with the goal of maximizing the wealth of its shareholders. Yet it is also true that shareholders would benefit by the removal of book-value constraints, because these constraints are likely to impede the goal of wealth maximization.

The upshot is that market values matter but book values may matter also. This means that a bank's lending decisions may be affected by its exposure to the borrower relative to either the market *or* the book value of its capacity to bear loss. The relevant concept may depend on the bank and the circumstances. We therefore look at the two cases separately when examining the lending-decision process.

4 The Capacity to Bear Loss and the Lending Decision

Bailout Loans and Spontaneous Loans

We examine here decisions about two kinds of loans, "spontaneous" and "bailout." Spontaneous loans are made to borrowers that are successfully

[12] See Guttentag and Herring (1985b) for an analysis of the reaction of the interbank market to bad news about a borrowing bank.

servicing their old debt and are expected to continue to do so. Such borrowers can obtain the same market terms from new lenders as from the lenders to which they are already indebted. (We defer until section 7 a consideration of the theory of spontaneous lending.)

Spontaneous lending disappears when a borrower's ability to service outstanding indebtedness becomes doubtful. This is, of course, the situation that has confronted many developing countries since August 1982. Under such circumstances, a significant part of the expected return on a new loan is the improved prospect that the borrower will repay its outstanding indebtedness. This is a bailout loan. Since lenders without previous exposure do not benefit from the improved repayment prospects of the borrower, they will not participate in bailout loans.[13]

Bailout Loans and Provisioning

Casual observation indicates that banks that have voluntarily accumulated substantial reserves or made comparable charge-offs against their cross-border loans to certain countries are often the most reluctant to make bailout loans to these countries. But this does not necessarily mean that the reserves or charge-offs cause the reluctance to make new loans. We will see later that a bank's willingness both to extend a bailout loan and to make provisions against, or charge off, old loans is influenced by its exposure to a borrowing country. "Exposure" refers to the maximum potential loss if the borrower does not repay. Exposure is usually measured in book values, although in some contexts the market value of exposure is more relevant.

If a bank is concerned that the book value of its capacity to bear loss is close to the regulatory minimum or is low relative to its peers, it is likely to be much more reluctant to make provisions or charge-offs than banks with a larger book capacity to bear loss. Also, if a bank's exposure to the borrower is smaller than that of its peers, it is more likely to make provisions or charge-offs as a way of calling attention to its lesser vulnerability to a default.[14] Thus, both the tendency to accumulate reserves or make charge-offs and the disinclination to make new loans may be the consequence of relatively small exposure. Yet we also see later that, under some circumstances, provisions

---

[13] This problem could be alleviated if a new lender were able to obtain a prior claim against the borrower, but international lending agreements usually contain clauses that prevent this. Negative-pledge clauses prevent the borrower from subordinating the lender's claim in subsequent loan transactions, and *pari passu* clauses assure that any privileges accorded new creditors will be extended to old ones. These rules effectively freeze past lending relationships until the servicing of past loans no longer depends on new loans and spontaneous lending can be regenerated (Eaton et al., 1986, p. 494, and Stiglitz and Weiss, 1983, pp. 918-919).

[14] Several regional banks have gone out of their way to inform the market that they had zero exposure. One bank proudly advertised that its only offshore loans were to Nantucket.

against loans to specific countries may have an independent influence on the willingness to lend.

A model of bailout lending is required to determine the independent influence of provisioning, charge-offs, and reserves. This section is based on the model developed in the Appendix. (Readers who prefer an algebraic exposition may wish to skip this and the following section and read the Appendix.)

Two assumptions are maintained throughout this section:

1. Bankers, tax authorities, regulators, investors, and bank creditors ignore accounting magnitudes that differ from market values. The assumption that only market values matter provides a useful benchmark against which, in the next section, we can assess the implications of assuming that accounting values also matter.
2. There is only one lender. While this assumption is manifestly inapplicable to contemporary debt-servicing problems, where the challenge of achieving collective action is very important, it is convenient to consider the simpler case before proceeding to the more complex one examined in section 6.

The analysis begins with three additional assumptions that are relaxed in sequence:

3. The bank's capacity to bear loss exceeds its outstanding claim against the borrower plus the bailout loan. (Thus, the bank would not fail if the bailout loan was unsuccessful.)
4. The bank is not subject to constraining capital requirements or to penalties if the book value of capital falls.
5. The bank maximizes expected profits (i.e., it is not subject to any risk constraint).

The Basic Case

Given these assumptions, a bank will be more willing to make a bailout loan (a) the higher the probability that the loan—along with the bank's old claim against the borrower—will be repaid, (b) the higher the spread on the new loan over the risk-free rate, and (c) the larger the bank's old claim against the borrower.

Obviously, the better the prospects that the borrower will repay, the greater the willingness of the bank to make the bailout loan. This probability depends on a number of factors, including macroeconomic conditions in the world economy and in the borrowing country (which are taken as given for our purposes). But the probability of success also depends on whether a large enough bailout loan is made. We focus on the probability of repayment asso-

16

ciated with the size of the bailout loan that yields the maximum probability of success[15] and defer until section 6 the question of whether a loan of optimal size can be mobilized.

Given all the other factors, a bank will be more willing to make a bailout loan when the contractual value of its outstanding claims on the borrower is large, because the recovery of those claims is part of the return on the bailout loan. This is a fundamental difference between spontaneous and bailout lending. In spontaneous lending, either a bank is indifferent to the amount of its outstanding claims against the borrower or, if it is risk-constrained, its willingness to make new loans will *decline* as the volume of its old claims rises.

To the extent that a bailout loan to one borrower is perceived to affect the probability that some of the bank's other borrowers will repay outstanding loans, the relevant measure of outstanding claims may be much larger than the claims on the specific borrower seeking a new loan. Such interconnections may be economic or political.

In this basic model of bailout lending, provisions and reserves do not matter, because they do not affect any of the factors that determine a bank's willingness to lend. The same is true of charge-offs. Although the contractual value of outstanding claims does influence the willingness to make new loans, the *accounting* value of such claims is irrelevant. What matters for the lending decision is the maximum amount the bank can collect from the borrower if the borrower is able and willing to repay the debt in full. Charge-offs affect this magnitude only if accompanied by explicit debt forgiveness.[16] In the absence of forgiveness, a bank's claim on the borrower is reduced only if the outstanding balance is repaid or the claim is sold.[17]

When the Bank Is Overexposed

If the bank's economic exposure to the borrower plus the bailout loan required to maximize the probability of repayment exceeds the bank's capacity to bear loss, the bank may be more willing to extend a bailout loan than in the basic case where the bank's capacity to bear loss is larger. The reason is that shareholders will obtain the full benefit if the bailout loan is

---

[15] See the first section of the Appendix for further discussion of this assumption.

[16] This point was emphasized by the Bank of Boston when it wrote off $200 million of its $1 billion of claims on developing countries. A spokesman for the bank said that the bank "fully expects the borrowers to repay their loans" (Financial Times, 1987, p. 359).

[17] The repurchase of outstanding obligations at a discount has been a feature of the resolution of several past debt crises (see Sachs, 1982). The volume of swaps and outright sales, which often permit the debtor to buy back its obligation at a discount, has substantially increased since Citicorp's special provision.

successful; if it fails, the part of the loss that exceeds the shareholders' equity will be borne by creditors or insurers.[18] Thus, the ability to shift potential losses to third parties increases the willingness to lend.

Countries with large absolute amounts of outstanding debt should find it easier to obtain bailout loans whether or not the bank is overexposed. As shown in Table 7, Brazil and Mexico, the two countries with the largest indebtedness to banks in 1982, accounted for $10 billion of the $11.8 billion increase in outstanding loans to public borrowers and banks in Latin America from 1982 to 1987.[19]

The modified model also implies that banks with greater exposures relative to capital should be more willing to make bailout loans. This is also consistent with the evidence shown in Table 7. The 9 money-center banks that had the highest ratios of exposure to capital in 1982, and also in 1987, accounted for all of the increase in outstanding loans to Latin American countries. (The increase in the claims of the 13 other large banks just offset the decrease in the claims of the nearly 200 smaller banks included in the Country Exposure Lending Survey.)

We do not know whether bailout lending decisions were influenced by the expectation that part of the risk of loss would be borne by third parties. Yet exposures relative to economic capacity to bear loss were very large for major U.S. banks after the debt crisis erupted. The book-value exposures to *all* Latin American borrowers for nine money-center banks in December 1982 was 172.5 percent of their primary capital. As we note later, basing both numerator and denominator on market values would not generate very different figures. Since the repayment prospects of these countries appeared to be highly interrelated (subsequent movements in secondary-market prices of claims on these countries have been highly correlated), the possibility cannot be disregarded that the banks viewed them as a single exposure.

As in the basic case, charge-offs will not affect the willingness to make new loans because of the assumption that changing the accounting value of exposure does not affect the bank's claims against the borrower, but provisioning that increases the bank's capacity to bear loss may do so. When exposure to

---

[18] This assumes that the third parties do not foresee that the bank is shifting an additional risk onto them and therefore fail to charge an appropriate risk premium. This assumption seems reasonable because most creditors of large banks are implicitly (though not explicitly) protected by deposit insurance, and the deposit insurance agency charges a premium that does not vary with the perceived riskiness of the institution. (See Buser, Chen, and Kane, 1981, for an argument that bank supervision may substitute in part for risk-sensitive deposit-insurance premiums.)

[19] Table 7 shows Country Exposure Lending Survey claims on public borrowers and banks, which provide a better measure of concerted lending than claims on the nonbank private sector.

TABLE 7

OUTSTANDING LOANS TO PUBLIC BORROWERS AND BANKS, 1982 AND 1987
(*in millions of dollars*)

	All U.S. Banks			9 Money-Center Banks		
	6/82	12/87	Change	6/82	12/87	Change
Total Latin America	$49,841	$ 61,594	$11,753	$29,282	$41,078	$11,796
Brazil	13,401	18,422	5,021	7,652	12,738	5,086
Mexico	13,185	18,227	5,042	7,809	11,115	3,306
Venezuela	6,931	7,188	257	4,674	5,183	509
Argentina	5,165	7,326	2,161	2,949	5,220	2,271
Chile	4,395	5,538	1,143	2,188	3,681	1,493
Peru	1,994	818	(1,176)	1,156	425	(731)
Colombia	1,720	1,689	(31)	1,090	1,160	70
Others	3,050	2,386	(664)	1,764	1,556	(208)
Total bank capital	$66,200	$129,000		$27,100	$51,500	
Total claims as a % of primary capital	75%	48%		108%	80%	

	13 Other Large Banks			Other Smaller Banks		
	6/82	12/87	Change	6/82	12/87	Change
Total Latin America	$ 9,401	$10,820	$1,419	$11,158	$9,696	($1,462)
Brazil	2,743	3,149	406	3,003	2,535	(468)
Mexico	1,927	3,192	1,265	3,449	3,920	471
Venezuela	1,228	1,274	46	1,029	731	(298)
Argentina	1,251	1,313	62	965	793	(172)
Chile	912	983	71	1,296	874	(422)
Peru	502	246	(256)	336	147	(189)
Colombia	335	295	(40)	294	234	(60)
Others	503	368	(135)	786	462	(324)
Total bank capital	$12,700	$ 3,900		$ 6,400	$3,800	
Total claims as a % of primary capital	74%	45%		42%	18%	

SOURCE: Country Exposure Lending Survey, Dec. 6, 1982, and Apr. 22, 1988.

the borrower plus the necessary bailout loan exceeds the bank's capacity to bear loss, increases in its capacity to bear loss may diminish its willingness to extend a bailout loan. Since the exposure of money-center banks to all Latin American borrowers had fallen (in book-value terms) to 95 percent by December 1987, a decreasing willingness to make bailout loans should not be surprising, even if the borrowers' prospects for repayment had not deteriorated.

Risk Neutrality

The assumption that banks maximize expected profits implies that they attach no cost to the variance of their total profits.[20] The assumption of risk-neutral bank behavior is widely used and defended. Tobin (1982, p. 523), for example, has observed:

> Risk-neutrality seems the appropriate assumption for the firm. A bank is managed by specialists engaged in taking a long sequence of risks . . . and can expect bad luck and good luck to "average out." That is, the long-run variance of the profits associated with any given policy is much smaller than the short-run variance.

Special circumstances, however, may lead to risk-averse behavior: (1) The bank may be closely held by managers who cannot diversify because the bank is the major part of their human and financial capital. This would be unusual among the major banks that are heavily involved in international lending but may be relevant to some small banks. (2) Shareholders may prefer that the bank minimize the risk of bankruptcy because they would lose the going-concern value of the bank (or be subject to some other default penalty) if it were to be closed (Herring and Vankudre, 1987). (3) Risk-averse managers who perceive that their jobs may be jeopardized by sharp declines in bank profits may impose a risk constraint to protect themselves. Even though shareholders might prefer that the bank maximize expected profits, monitoring costs may give managers some scope for pursuing their own interests. (4) Bank-supervisory authorities may constrain the bank's risk in order to reduce the possibility of bankruptcy or prevent the bank from taking undue advantage of deposit insurance or emergency liquidity assistance.

If a bank's objective is to maximize expected profits subject to a binding constraint that the probability the bank will fail does not exceed some specified level, increases in the bank's capacity to bear loss tend to relax the constraint. A larger capacity to bear loss allows the bank to make loans that increase the anticipated variance of profits to levels that would have been unacceptable before. The bank could therefore make bailout loans that it was previously constrained from making.

Presumably, this case would apply only to a bank that was not overexposed. A bank with an exposure larger than its capacity to bear loss is undoubtedly in violation of any risk constraint it may have had. We have shown elsewhere (Guttentag and Herring, 1986a) how this could happen. The excessive risk exposure of such a bank is unintentional, reflecting prior mistakes or unanticipated bad luck. This may be the explanation for the predicament of several heavily exposed U.S. banks.

---

[20] This assumption does not imply that bank shareholders are also risk neutral: risk-averse shareholders can reduce variance in their own income by diversifying their portfolios.

How does a bank behave after it has unintentionally violated its self-imposed risk constraint and cannot honor it immediately without going out of business? This is an unexplored theoretical question. Our surmise is that a bank would try to generate retained earnings as rapidly as possible in order to satisfy its risk constraint once again. But the quickest way of generating reserves internally is to maximize expected profits. Thus the risk constraint becomes irrelevant to the bailout-lending decision, and—just as in the case where the bank is risk neutral—increases in the bank's capacity to bear loss will reduce the willingness to make such a loan.

5 The Lending Decision When Book Values Matter

Book capacity to bear loss, as opposed to economic capacity to bear loss, may be important when book values affect market perceptions, regulatory actions, management compensation, or tax payments. In such cases, book capacity to bear loss may also affect the willingness of a bank to make new bailout loans.

Book Values and the Incentive to Make Bailout Loans

When bank managers perceive a cost in *reporting* a decline in the value of an asset, the incentive to make a bailout loan is enhanced. A bailout loan gives the bank a chance not only to retrieve its outstanding claims on the borrower but to delay—perhaps indefinitely—charging off its outstanding exposure by enabling the borrower to stay current on interest payments. Indeed, if new loans do not exceed accumulated interest, the bank can accomplish this without increasing its exposure.

In the Appendix, we assume that the bank perceives a cost to reducing the stated value of claims on the borrower that is proportional to the book value of those claims. This becomes part of the cost of *not* making the bailout loan, since the outstanding exposure must be charged off if the bailout loan is not made. The cost is also a negative component of the expected return on the bailout loan: if the bailout loan fails, both it and the outstanding exposure must be charged off. But the cost is certain if the loan is not made (a probability weight equal to 1), while the failure of the bailout loan is uncertain (a probability weight less than 1). Thus, on balance there is an increased incentive to make the bailout loan.

Voluntary Provisioning and Charge-Offs

When book values matter, an increase in book capacity to bear loss will reduce the incentive to make a bailout loan even if economic capacity is not affected. It reduces the perceived cost of recording reductions in asset values that could be avoided by making the loan. In our model, this cost is assumed to be inversely proportional to the difference between current book capacity to bear loss and that level of book capacity which would trigger adverse reactions from creditors or regulators.

In addition, charge-offs and provisions against loans to a specific borrower may reduce the expected return on bailout loans to that borrower, for two reasons. First, specific provisions or charge-offs reduce the decline in reported income or asset values that would occur if the loan were *not* made. Second, accountants (or regulators) may require similar provisions or charge-offs on new loans to that borrower. Accountants usually require that new medium-term credits in support of balance-of-payments adjustment programs be treated no differently from outstanding claims on the same borrower. If there are provisions against the old loans, they will be required on the new loan as well, unless the new loan can be construed as a prior claim on the borrower's resources. Thus a bank that has taken a 50 percent specific provision against its loans to a particular country has halved the potential drop in its book capacity to bear loss that would occur if it did not make a bailout loan, and it may be obliged to make a 50 percent provision if it *does* make a bailout loan.[21]

Mandatory Specific Provisions

The same problem arises in the case of mandatory specific provisions that oblige banks to credit special liability accounts in amounts equal to some percentage of their total claims against a specified country or "basket" of countries. Unless supervisors and regulators change requirements as soon as a borrower's prospects change or exempt new loans from old requirements, mandatory provisioning will reduce the expected return from new loans.

In Canada, Japan, the Netherlands, Spain, Sweden, and Switzerland, the requirement is specified against one basket or several baskets of debtor countries. The number of baskets ranges from one in Japan and Canada to five in Spain. The fewer the baskets and the larger the number of debtors in any one basket, the less sensitive the provisioning rule is likely to be to improvement in the status of any one debtor.

In some countries, the rule is completely mechanical; for example, the basket might include all loans to every debtor that has undergone a rescheduling exercise over the previous five years. In such a case, even a dramatic improvement in a debtor's economic condition will not relax provisioning requirements on new loans.

---

[21] Ordinarily, a bank would not voluntarily make provisions that would constrain it from making loans it wanted to make, but foresight is imperfect. After the provision is taken, the bank's managers may find that the condition of a borrower has unexpectedly improved. Nevertheless, reversal of provisions usually requires that the borrower's credit standing be completely restored; partial restoration is not sufficient.

The Bank of England (1987) has taken a more flexible approach. Each debtor country is given a risk rating based on fifteen factors, and an appropriate level of loan-loss reserves is indicated for each of five ranges of the risk rating. Changes in circumstances of individual debtors are reflected in changes in ratings that lead automatically to changes in the suggested level of reserves.

In the United States, reserve requirements against individual countries are also relatively flexible. The U.S. authorities have been careful to exempt certain categories of new lending from the ATTR requirement,[22] and they have made clear their intention to revise the classification of a country as soon as conditions warrant. (Turkey is the most notable case of a country that has been upgraded.) Flexibility imposes a burden of discretion on the U.S. authorities, and it may subject them to political pressures to revise classifications prematurely or to delay adverse classifications unduly.

6 Provisioning and the Collective-Action Problem

To this point we have assumed that total claims against a country are held by one lender. In fact, many lenders are involved, and the need for collective action is an important problem. After a brief review of the problem (for a more extensive discussion, see Herring, 1989), we focus on how provisioning affects prospects for achieving collective action.

The problem of collective action arises when no individual lender has an incentive to make the full bailout loan unilaterally but lenders have a collective interest in the borrower's receiving the loan. The larger the number of individual lenders, the smaller the incentive for any one lender to take action in the collective interest and the greater the difficulties in achieving collective action.

This means that the model of bailout lending developed above, which assumes a single lender, indicates the *maximum* volume of lending that could be expected in a regime of many lenders. The actual volume of lending will approach that maximum insofar as individual lenders are induced to behave in the collective interest.

There are bargaining costs inherent in obtaining agreement among a large number of independent decision-makers. Furthermore, anticipation of the difficulty of achieving collective action may discourage individual lenders from participating. An individual lender's expectation that a bailout loan will succeed depends not only on the lender's perception of the borrower's ability and willingness to repay but also on the expected behavior of other creditors.

---

[22] These categories are usually short-term credits. Thus far, the supervisory authorities have found it difficult to exempt medium-term credits, which are most useful for supporting balance-of-payments adjustment programs.

If a bank expects other lenders to opt out, it will assign the bailout loan a lower probability of success than if it can count on each lender to contribute a proportional share. Anticipation of difficulty in organizing a bailout loan may become a self-fulfilling prophecy.

Another impediment is that individual banks may expect a free ride on a bailout loan made by other lenders. A bank is more likely to expect a free ride if it believes that other lenders will be willing to make bailout loans larger than their shares of the outstanding claims on the borrower. There may be political reasons for official entities to grant subsidies or extend bailout loans to the borrower, or other lenders may be known to be much more heavily exposed.

The difficulty of achieving collective action increases with differences among the banks regarding the variety of factors that bear on their willingness to make bailout loans. Some banks, for example, have important collateral relationships with the debtor that would be jeopardized if the bailout loan failed. Some banks have more leeway than others to deduct provisions or charge-offs from taxable income, and some place greater value on international cooperation. But the most important difference among the banks may be the extent of their exposure relative to their capacity to bear loss. Among other things, the greater the differences in exposure, the more severe the free-rider problem. Furthermore, some banks with relatively small exposure may believe they can obtain a competitive advantage vis-à-vis more heavily exposed banks if the bailout loan is not made and the more heavily exposed banks are thus forced to reduce the book value of their capacity to bear loss (and perhaps be subject to regulatory sanctions).

While exposure has declined and capacity to bear loss has risen for most banks since 1982, this trend has been much more pronounced for the banks that were less exposed in 1982. In addition, banks with relatively small exposure appear to have made much larger specific balance-sheet provisions than have banks with larger exposure. On the assumption that book values matter to the first group of banks, these provisions have further reduced the return to them from bailout lending, for reasons discussed earlier.

Consequently, trends in exposure relative to capacity to bear loss, as well as in specific provisioning, have caused the perceived returns on bailout loans to decline more for banks that faced relatively low expected returns in 1982 because of their relatively small exposure. These trends have increased the difference in expected returns on bailout loans between the heavily exposed and lightly exposed banks and have thus made collective action more difficult.[23]

---

[23] One factor could work in the opposite direction. The most exposed banks in 1982 may have been *overexposed* in the sense that their potential losses exceeded their economic capacity to

7 The Impact of Provisioning and Charge-Offs on Spontaneous Lending

Spontaneous loans are made only to borrowers in good standing that are expected to remain in good standing. The hallmark of a spontaneous loan is that it yields the same expected return to lenders that already have claims on the borrower as to lenders that do not. Since the borrower is expected to service outstanding claims on time, whatever the decision of existing creditors regarding a new loan, the repayment of outstanding exposure is not part of the lender's expected return on a spontaneous loan. By the same token, historical book values play no role in the new lending decision.

Provisioning has two kinds of effect on spontaneous lending. The mandatory specific provisioning rules that were adopted after 1982 are relatively unimportant among the many factors that have reduced the expected return on spontaneous loans. In contrast, provisioning that increases the capacity to bear loss may in time encourage spontaneous lending by relaxing the risk constraints that may deter some banks.

Factors Depressing the Expected Return on Spontaneous Loans

Probably the most important reason for the decline in spontaneous lending after 1982 was the sharp decline in the expected return on cross-border loans to many developing countries. We have argued (in Guttentag and Herring, 1986a) that, before the Mexican debt crisis in August 1982, expected returns were overestimated, for a number of reasons:

1. Banks may have been subject to disaster myopia regarding the possibility of major shocks carrying low, but unknown, probabilities.
2. Banks may have placed undue reliance on the efficacy of short maturities to protect themselves against debt-servicing difficulties.
3. Banks may have believed that governments or international institutions would protect them against severe loss if debt-servicing problems affected most major banks.
4. Banks may have made excessively optimistic inferences from inadequate data concerning the current condition and outstanding indebtedness of major countries.

Payment interruptions on sovereign debt since August 1982 have deflated these optimistic assumptions regarding the probability of default. Indeed, the same factors that gave rise to disaster myopia before 1982 may lead to overestimates of the probability of default on spontaneous loans. Short maturities have provided uncertain protection, and in some instances they have been rescheduled on the same basis as other debt. (Indeed, in one instance only short-term claims were rescheduled.) The implicit guarantees

---

bear loss. If this is no longer true, a major source of difference between the banks has been removed.

anticipated from governments and international agencies have so far proved disappointing. And, in the wake of one unpleasant surprise after another, inadequate data are now interpreted pessimistically rather than optimistically.

The regulatory response to the debt crisis since 1982 is also likely to retard the resumption of spontaneous lending. Banks in most countries have been pressured to increase their capacity to bear loss. Higher capital-asset ratios increase the required rate of return on all assets subject to the ratio and thus harden the terms on which new loans will be made. Many countries have put systems into place to include cross-border loans in evaluations of capital adequacy and to impose mandatory provisions against troubled foreign debt. These measures are an abrupt departure from the earlier era, when cross-border loans were not subject to special regulatory provisions.

Cross-border loans are also subject to far greater public disclosure. The public reaction that preceded and accompanied many of these regulatory measures is perhaps even more harmful to prospects for a resumption of spontaneous lending than the regulatory measures themselves. In the United States, particularly, banks were subjected to heavy political attack for allegedly wasting money abroad while domestic needs were unsatisfied. As a consequence, banks may demand a higher expected return from new foreign loans to compensate for potential political costs.

Finally, the wave of deregulation sweeping around the world is giving banks access to new activities and new markets in countries with high per capita incomes. It is generally anticipated that the expected return on loans and investments in the advanced industrial countries will be much higher than in the era before 1982. This will increase the opportunity cost of loans to developing countries.

The Impact of Provisioning on Risk Constraints

When banks are risk-constrained, the outstanding exposure to a given country has a negative impact on the willingness to make new loans to that country even when the old loans are in good standing. (Guttentag and Herring, 1986c, present a formal analysis of one such model.) The impact is greater the larger the anticipated covariance with the rest of the portfolio and the smaller the bank's capacity to bear loss. Hence, given the risk constraint, increases in capacity to bear loss increase the willingness to make new loans.

We have argued (Guttentag and Herring, 1985c) that before 1982 banks underestimated the correlation of risks among loans to different countries, believing that their portfolios of cross-border loans were highly diversified. They tended to ignore systematic linkages associated with (a) potential increases in real interest rates that would affect all borrowing countries and (b) potential funding problems that would face developing countries in the event of a deterioration of confidence in their creditworthiness. These mistakes will not soon be repeated. In view of the recent unfavorable experience, there may even be a tendency to exaggerate such linkages. Mandatory provisioning requirements against loans to baskets of developing countries, implying as they do that the countries in a basket are linked, may reinforce this tendency.

Large anticipated covariances among a group of loans that constitute a significant proportion of a bank's capital may deter new lending to individual countries within the group even though each exposure considered separately is a small proportion of total capital. Under such circumstances, provisioning should increase the bank's willingness to make new loans, because it enables the bank to accept a higher degree of exposure or covariance and still remain within its risk constraint.

Ironically, the negative short-run impact of specific provisioning on the willingness to make bailout loans may have a positive effect on the willingness of a risk-constrained bank to resume spontaneous lending in the long run. With loans to developing countries static, the growth of the rest of the bank's portfolio gradually reduces the covariance of the return on new loans to developing countries with the return on the rest of the portfolio. We would view any such effect, however, as of very small importance relative to the powerful forces operating in the other direction.

8 Citicorp's Decision

On May 19, 1987, Citicorp announced a provision of $3 billion against its loans to thirty-one less developed countries that had been experiencing debt-servicing difficulties.[24] Citicorp was not the first major bank to allocate a substantial provision against possible losses on restructured sovereign debt, nor was its reserve the largest relative to its outstanding loans.[25] But Citicorp's action surely had the most dramatic impact, partly because it was the largest single holder of claims on developing countries and partly because it had played a leading role in most debt renegotiations.

---

[24] The thirty-one countries are Argentina, Bolivia, Brazil, Chile, Costa Rica, Dominican Republic, Ecuador, Gabon, Honduras, Ivory Coast, Jamaica, Liberia, Malagasy, Malawi, Mexico, Morocco, Mozambique, Nicaragua, Nigeria, Panama, Peru, Philippines, Poland, Senegal, South Africa, Sudan, Uruguay, Venezuela, Yugoslavia, Zaire, and Zambia. This list does not include all countries whose debt sells at a discount on secondary markets. For example, Colombia does not appear on the list, even though its claims sold for a 34 percent discount in May 1988. Colombia does not meet Citibank's criterion of having rescheduled its external bank debt.

[25] For example, Deutsche Bank was reported to have established a reserve of 70 percent of outstanding exposure, in comparison with Citicorp's reserve of 25 percent.

Accounting Aspects

Citicorp (1988, p. 31) indicated that the provision would be identified with (but not limited to) claims on the thirty-one countries:

> Since all identified losses are immediately written off, no portion of the allowance is specifically allocated or restricted to any individual loan or group of loans, and the entire allowance is available to absorb any and all credit losses. However, for analytical purposes, Citicorp views its allowances as attributable to . . . [these countries].

Citicorp's rationale for identifying the provision with a group of specified countries was that this would strengthen its strategic position in subsequent negotiations with some of these countries, a point developed later. In addition, the bank's new management team may have wished to separate itself from earlier mistakes by making a cleaner accounting distinction between earnings from current operating performance and losses inherited from the past. Finally, Citicorp may have believed that if it did not voluntarily set aside a substantial reserve against developing-country debt, it might soon be obliged to do so, since a number of proposals mandating special reserves had been introduced in Congress.

Citicorp's rationale for not allocating the reserves to individual countries was that this would have prevented it from including the reserves as part of the general loan-loss reserve that is counted as part of primary capital by U.S. regulatory authorities. Furthermore, if the bank had made specific rather than general provisions, it might have reduced its freedom to treat new loans to the thirty-one countries more favorably in its financial statements than it treated existing claims.

Indeed, Citicorp may have believed that its action would strengthen the resolve of U.S. authorities to continue to include loan-loss reserves in the regulatory definition of capital. At the time, the U.S. authorities were developing a new framework to regulate capital adequacy with their counterparts from eleven other countries in the Basle Committee on Bank Regulation and Supervisory Practices, and the issue of how to treat loan-loss reserves was under discussion. (In the event, a compromise was reached on this issue. The proposed regulations released in January 1988 include loan-loss reserves as part of second-tier capital. But by the end of 1992, when the new approach is scheduled to be fully implemented, loan-loss reserves will be counted in second-tier capital only up to an amount equal to 1.25 percent of risk-weighted assets.)

Within weeks of Citicorp's announcement, most other major U.S. banks that had not already done so established a comparable reserve (see Table 1, column 1, above). Subsequently, all the major banks in the United Kingdom and Canada followed suit. Why was this action taken when it was, and what are the likely consequences for bailout lending and a resumption of spontaneous lending?

Citicorp's Official Explanation

Citicorp was obliged to explain to the SEC why it had suddenly reduced the value of its claims on troubled debtors by such a large amount. The SEC often takes a skeptical view of sudden announcements of a decline in the value of corporate assets if there is reason to believe the decline could have been anticipated earlier. The formal SEC filing, the Form 8-K announcing an unusual event, contained a one-sentence explanation:

> [The provision was made] to reflect the increasingly visible economic reality that the adjustment process for the heavily indebted countries will stretch into the 1990's, the impairment of this portfolio as seen in the recent agreements and the current events in Brazil, and the decision by Citicorp to restructure its exposure through debt-equity swaps, sales and other actions (Jones, 1987, p. 2).

The banks that filed after Citicorp found it much easier to justify the timing of their special provisions because they could cite Citicorp's action.

The SEC chose not to quibble over this sentence; presumably, it saw no useful purpose in asking Citicorp (and all the major banks that followed) to restate their earnings for previous years.

Changing Attitudes toward Repayment Prospects

In its terse explanation, Citicorp acknowledged that it had modified its views regarding repayment prospects. Until the second quarter of 1987, Citicorp and most other U.S. banks with heavy concentrations of claims on troubled debtor countries had shown great reluctance to make provisions against sovereign debt, insisting that sovereign loans were ultimately collectable. The general strategy was to treat the debt-servicing problems of major debtor countries as if they were liquidity problems that would ease when the debtors initiated policy reforms and when growth in the world economy reverted to the trend in earlier decades. In most cases, troubled debtor countries were given only enough new loans to permit them to stay current on interest payments.

The wait-and-see policy had a double rationale. On the one hand, it avoided the need to make a definitive disposition of claims on the debtor countries until events had demonstrated that the claims were uncollectable. At the same time, it gave the most heavily exposed banks time to grow out of the problem by increasing their capacity to bear loss through earnings retention while capping growth in exposure.

Although most of the major creditor banks grew stronger after 1982, most of the debtor countries did not, and the assumption that their debt-servicing problems were temporary grew less and less tenable. The secondary market in country loans became an increasingly cited indicator that the ultimate collectability of many sovereign loans was in doubt (see Figure 2). The banks continued to argue that the secondary market was extremely thin and not representative of informed expectations regarding the prospects of the major debtors, but the argument was undercut by the fact that no major bank was buying loans even at what were purported to be fire-sale prices.[26]

FIGURE 2
INDEX OF THE SECONDARY-MARKET VALUE OF THE DEBT
OF REFINANCING COUNTRIES, 1986-87

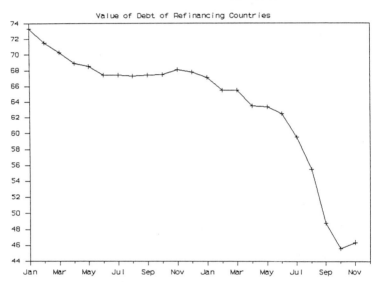

NOTE: The index is a weighted average value of the outstanding commercial-bank debt of Argentina, Brazil, Chile, Colombia, Ecuador, Mexico, Peru, and the Philippines, Poland, Romania, Venezuela, and Yugoslavia, based upon the average price of actual transactions completed by Shearson Lehman during the preceding month.

SOURCE: *Financial Times* (1987).

The low price-earnings multiples of banks with heavy exposure to sovereign debt relative to regional banks with negligible exposure and to nonbank corporations implied that the stock market's view of the value of sovereign loans was closer to that of the secondary market than to the value carried on the books of the banks. At least one influential bank security analyst, more-

[26] While the secondary market in sovereign loans is undoubtedly very imperfect, it is not clear that the factors causing downward bias in market prices outweigh those causing upward bias (GAO, 1988, p.29).

over, wrote about the need to make provisions against troubled sovereign debt and published estimates of the impact on several major banks of provisions equal to the difference between the book value and secondary-market value of sovereign loans (Hanley et al., 1987).

Perhaps of greater importance, official policy in the United States and other major creditor countries was evolving toward an acceptance of the possibility that the problems of the developing countries were not transient. In the fall of 1986, public officials in creditor countries had pressed the banks to restructure Mexico's bank debt on terms that many banks thought too lenient. Several banks ultimately refused to sign the agreement, and John Reed, the chairman of Citicorp, was reported to have accepted it only with the greatest reluctance (Truell, 1987).

Early in January 1987, the *Washington Post* and the *Financial Times* reported that U.S. Secretary of the Treasury James Baker had indicated that American banks might be obliged to accept losses on loans to major Latin American debtors. An unnamed Treasury official was quoted as saying that "the debt is not worth 100 cents on the dollar and we should not be engaging in the fiction that it is" (Fleming, 1987). This was the first time a senior U.S. official had raised the possibility publicly. Although the reports were subsequently denied, many observers inferred that the administration was reconsidering its firm opposition to policies that would result in charging off sovereign debt. Moreover, a number of proposals were introduced in Congress that would require provisions, reserves, and charge-offs of third-world debt as part of a broader solution to the debt problem.

Relations between banks and some of the major debtor countries were deteriorating. During February 1987, Brazil—the developing country with the largest external debt—declared a moratorium on interest payments to banks. This was an especially serious blow to Citicorp, which had more loans outstanding to Brazil than any other bank, an amount equal to 34.1 percent of its primary capital (Truell, 1987).

In sum, by the second quarter of 1987, after almost five years of frustrating debt renegotiations, Citicorp was more or less forced to acknowledge that losses on claims against the thirty-one countries were probable. But by then Citicorp, along with most other major banks, was in a much stronger position to recognize the losses. This was an important factor bearing on Citicorp's decision that was *not* acknowledged in its SEC statement. Table 8 shows how the book value of Citicorp's equity would have been affected if it had taken the $3 billion provision earlier.[27] Although U.S. capital requirements do not specify a minimum ratio of equity capital to assets, bank examiners and bank

---

[27] Note that some other major banks would have entirely exhausted the book value of their equity if they had written down a comparable proportion of their claims in 1982.

TABLE 8

NET INCOME OF CITICORP, NOTIONALLY ADJUSTED
FOR A $3 BILLION PROVISION

Year End	Net Income (1)	Book Value of Equity (2)	Adjusted Book Value of Equity [a] (3)	Assets Year End (4)	Equity-to-Asset Ratio (2) / (4)	Adjusted Equity-to-Asset Ratio (3) / (4)
1982	$ 723	$4,815	$2,538	$129,997	3.70%	1.95%
1983	860	5,771	3,631	134,655	4.29%	2.70%
1984	890	6,426	4,316	150,586	4.27%	2.87%
1985	998	7,765	5,763	173,597	4.47%	3.32%
1986	1,058	9,060	7,118	196,124	4.62%	3.63%
1987	(1,138)	8,810 [b]	8,810	203,607	4.33% [b]	4.33%

[a] The actual book value of equity is adjusted to reflect the impact on the book value of equity if a $3 billion provision had been taken that year.

[b] The 1987 figures represent the $3 billion provision actually taken.

SOURCE: Citicorp Annual Reports.

security analysts generally expect a sound bank to have equity equal to at least half of its primary capital. From this perspective, it would have been awkward for Citicorp to sustain the loss of book equity before 1986. By 1987, it was able to do so and still have an equity-to-asset ratio that exceeded its ratio in 1982.

Declines in Exposure Relative to the Capacity to Bear Loss

A better indication of the ability of major banks to absorb a balance-sheet "hit" is the trend in their exposure relative to their capacity to bear loss. Table 9 shows that Citicorp's exposure to four major Latin American borrowers declined slightly after 1982 but that its exposure relative to the book value of its equity or primary capital declined sharply.

Neither of these measures takes account of information provided by the market on the value of the bank's equity and the value of its developing-country loans. A third measure corrects this deficiency. It relates the secondary-market value of the bank's Latin American claims to the market value of the bank's equity.[28] These data indicate that the ratio of the market value

[28] The secondary-market value of the bank's Latin American claims is a very crude estimate. In addition to the limitations of secondary-market prices already noted, it takes no account of differences in the kinds of claim held against a given country. For example, it does not distinguish trade credits from interbank claims or medium-term balance-of-payments loans.

TABLE 9

EXPOSURE OF CITICORP TO FOUR MAJOR LATIN AMERICAN BORROWERS

Year End	Book-Value Exposure				Market Value Exposure	
	Amount Net of External Guarantees	As a % of Primary Capital	As a % of Book Value of Equity	As a % of Market Value of Equity	Amount at Market Value	As a % of Market Value of Equity
1982	$10,823	195.04	224.31	261.87		
1983	10,350	157.10	179.35	203.02		
1984	10,300	116.10	160.29	189.48		
1985	10,100	92.73	130.07	133.39	$7,257	95.84
1986	9,800	72.65	108.17	113.93	6,504	75.61
1987	9,100	54.26	103.29	126.58	4,302	59.84

NOTES: Computations based on data in Citicorp Annual Reports, Hanley et al. (1988b), and Financial Times (1987). Market-value measures computed by multiplying Citibank's outstanding claims on the four countries by the corresponding secondary market price stated as a percentage of the face value of the claim.

of exposure to the market value of the capacity to bear loss declined sharply during 1985-87, the period for which secondary-market prices on developing-country debt are available. Thus, although Citicorp was still vulnerable to losses in 1986-87, it was much less vulnerable than when the crisis began in 1982.

For the nine money-center banks as a group, exposure data are available that cover seven debtor countries (see Table 10). The trend for all the banks is similar to that for Citicorp. The face value of the Latin American claims of the nine money-center banks declined slightly after 1982. Since these banks substantially increased the book value of their capacity to bear loss through 1986, the ratio of exposure to the book value of their capacity to bear loss declined, whether measured by primary capital or by the book value of equity.[29] A major reason for the wait-and-see approach in 1982-83 was to give the most heavily exposed banks an opportunity to "outgrow" the problem. This stratagem has been at least partly vindicated by events. Citicorp's example in taking substantial provisions was followed by the other major banks, in part because most (though not all) of them had, like Citicorp,

[29] Exposure as a percentage of book value rose during 1987 because the extraordinary loan-loss provisions reduced the book value of equity. Exposure as a percentage of market value rose during 1987 because the market value of equity was much lower after the stock-market decline at the end of October 1987.

33

TABLE 10

EXPOSURE OF NINE MAJOR BANKS TO SEVEN LATIN AMERICAN COUNTRIES

Year End	Book-Value				Market Value	
	Exposure Net of External Guarantees	As a % of Primary Capital	As a % of Book Value of Equity	As a % of Market Value of Equity	Exposure at Market Value	Exposure at Market as a % of Market Value of Equity
1982	$50,029	172.51	206.19	285.05		
1983	50,171	159.27	179.94	247.76		
1984	52,578	143.26	173.96	226.36		
1985	51,309	121.30	156.52	172.25	$36,293	121.84
1986	50,229	107.56	139.89	153.02	32,877	100.16
1987	48,835	94.83	153.28	193.51	24,059	95.34

SOURCE: Computations based on data in Country Exposure Lending Surveys, 1982-88; Hanley et al. (1988b); Keefe Equity Research (1987); and Financial Times (1987). Market-value measures of debt computed by multiplying the face values of claims one each of seven countries (Argentina, Brazil, Chile, Colombia, Mexico, Peru, and Venezuela) by the indicative prices. The aggregate was then rescaled to reflect the ratio of these seven countries to aggregate claims on all Latin American countries. This adjustment factor varied from 1.02 to 1.05.

improved their capacity to bear loss relative to exposure. Besides, markets had reacted very favorably to Citicorp's action. Creditors did not panic, and equity investors emphatically approved (for reasons discussed below). Furthermore, Citicorp had established an *accounting* precedent. If the bank holding the largest amount of claims had concluded that the claims were not worth full face value, other banks would be hard-pressed to convince their auditors that their own claims were more valuable. Bankers Trust, for example, stated that its provision was taken in light of recent developments, "most particularly the potential effects of the actions of other banks in increasing their loan loss allowances" (Denny, 1987).

Relaxation of Book-Value Constraints

A third motivation for Citicorp's decision was to relax the constraints on its operating freedom that were imposed by the need to consider the book-value implications of its actions. We noted earlier that a bank paying attention to book values may still be maximizing shareholder wealth if it perceives that creditors or regulators will react adversely to a decline in the book value of equity and reported income. Yet, clearly, a bank will do better for its shareholders if its balance-sheet position is strong enough to permit it to focus on economic values when they differ from book values. Rational bank managers will balance the benefits of greater operating flexibility against the dangers of adverse public and regulatory reactions.

Given the improvement in Citicorp's book-value position by 1987, the balance of advantage had evidently tipped to operating flexibility. Nevertheless, the risk was still considered consequential, as indicated by Citicorp's elaborate precautions to protect its liquidity in case the market response was adverse (Bartlett et al., 1987, p. 43). The bank was also careful to give prior notification to several key participants in the negotiating process with developing countries: the Federal Reserve, Treasury, and SEC were fully briefed before the announcement was made; the governments of important debtor countries were given hand-delivered explanations of the action at the time it was made public; and some banks with weak balance sheets and heavy exposure were informed so that they could make preparations to deal with possible adverse market reactions.

What specific benefits did Citicorp perceive from greater flexibility? Citicorp evidently wanted to toughen its negotiating stance with the debtor countries. It took great pains to reaffirm its commitment to play a leading role in implementing the Baker Plan (Treasury Secretary Baker's initiative establishing modest goals for new concerted lending by commercial banks in conjunction with increased official lending to the principal debtor countries). But it also made clear its displeasure with the trend in recent negotiations toward lower spreads, longer grace periods, and an increasing concentration of claims on public borrowers.

In several cases, debtor countries had attempted to take advantage of accounting rules regarding nonperforming loans to gain leverage in their negotiations with the banks. Because U.S. banks are required to reverse accrued interest when it becomes ninety days overdue, some countries deferred serious negotiations until just before that point. Their negotiators apparently believed that U.S. banks would be more likely to make concessions when faced with the prospect of reversing accrued interest. The Argentinean negotiation in 1984 was the most publicized but not the only example of this tactic. Moreover, creditor banks outside the United States were becoming increasingly annoyed that the negotiating process was being shaped by arbitrary U.S. accounting conventions, and the debtor-country negotiators may have seen an opportunity to drive a wedge between U.S. banks and other banks not facing similar accounting constraints.

When Brazil declared its moratorium on interest payments to banks early in 1987, Citicorp, along with several other major banks, quickly put Brazilian loans on a nonaccrual basis so that interest would be entered in the income statement only when received. The speed with which this action was taken—well before the interest was ninety days overdue—was widely interpreted as

35

a sign that banks were strengthening their cohesion and toughening their negotiating stance. It removed whatever bargaining leverage Brazil may have hoped to obtain from the ninety-day rule and demonstrated to Brazil that the banks were prepared to accept the loss of income rather than negotiate an unsatisfactory agreement. Citicorp's earnings dropped by $200 million (after taxes) during 1987 because of the Brazilian moratorium (Citicorp, 1988, p. 28).

The loan-loss provision was designed to make the point even more forcibly. It constituted an announcement that the bank was now in a position to sustain charge-offs if necessary. By placing the addition to the loan-loss reserve in a special category identified explicitly with claims on the debtor countries, Citicorp was emphasizing its willingness to absorb losses on that particular part of its balance sheet.

It has been argued that the increased bargaining leverage obtained by explicitly taking losses may have cost Citicorp (and other banks) support from creditor governments. Although those governments have a strong interest in the solvency of the banking system, their concern for its profitability is less intense. When bank solvency is no longer in jeopardy, governments will place greater emphasis on foreign-policy goals and the expansion of export markets. Yet it seems clear that government policy had begun to shift before Citicorp's announcement. Moreover, government policy is likely to be based on the banks' ability to absorb book losses rather than on whether they have increased their loan-loss reserves.

The loosening of book-value constraints also facilitated loan sales, debt-for-equity swaps, and other transformations of outstanding loans into other kinds of claims. This was particularly important to Citicorp because it could take advantage of its strong local presence in many of the most important debtor countries. Citicorp owns the largest bank in the Philippines, the only private bank in Mexico, two of the largest ten banks in Brazil, and significant banks in Argentina, Chile, and Venezuela. Citicorp quickly took advantage of its new accounting flexibility, reducing its outstanding claims on developing countries by $1.6 billion during 1987 and charging off $279 million of credit losses against the new reserve account (Citicorp, 1988, pp. 27 and 30).

Tax benefits may have been a factor as well. These were estimated at $400 to $500 million during 1987 and up to $600 million in future years.[30]

The stock market's highly favorable reaction to Citicorp's announcement was consistent with the view that depreciation in the value of the bank's claims was already fully reflected in its stock price and that the removal of

---

[30] The timing of the tax benefits is complex. The provisions are not deductible until actual charge-offs occur, and the charge-offs yield tax benefits only to the extent that they offset current tax liabilities or can be carried back to offset taxes paid in earlier years. It should be noted that, by increasing the tax liabilities of banks, the tax law that became effective in 1987 increased the incentive to reduce taxable income.

book-value constraints would allow it to improve its return to shareholders.[31] On the day after the announcement, Citicorp had an excess return over the general market of 4.7 percent (Musumeci and Sinkey, 1988).

The other money-center banks also had excess returns, with the exception of BankAmerica and Continental Illinois, which were probably viewed as unable to match Citicorp's provision without reducing the book value of equity to unacceptable levels.

9   Conclusion: The Future of Bank Lending to Developing Countries

What does the Citicorp episode presage for bank lending to developing countries? It is convenient to view this question in terms of developments in the capacity of banks to bear loss. The book value of the capacity to bear loss of the major banks increased appreciably from 1982 to 1987, both in absolute terms and relative to exposure. We have seen that the opportunity cost of not making bailout loans includes expected adverse consequences from a reduction in the book value of equity if the loan is not made, and that this cost falls as the book value of equity rises. Without taking into account any changes in perceptions regarding the future prospects of the countries involved, it follows that major banks probably became less willing to make bailout loans during this period. This development paved the way for the Citicorp announcement.

At first glance, Citicorp's announcement appeared to pertain merely to an accounting event: since the bank made a transfer from its equity account to its loan-loss reserve account and did not reduce its dividend, it did not increase the funds available to absorb a loss. But the announcement was more than an accounting event. With the similar actions by most other major banks, it made clear that the banks would no longer feel constrained by the need to protect the book values of their claims. Although the banks still have an enormous stake in those claims, the threat posed to the book-value solvency of the banks is not what it was. This implies that the banks will be less concerned to negotiate agreements that maintain the book value of their claims and will place greater emphasis on other options that seem more likely to increase the economic value of those claims. The favorable reaction of the stock market to the announcement indicated that investors believed this change in emphasis would enhance the profitability of banks.

Looking ahead, the removal of book-value constraints and the associated

---

[31] By contrast, the near-term impact on the secondary market for country loans was strongly negative (see Figure 2), presumably reflecting expectations of larger secondary-market sales by banks newly freed from their accounting constraints. *Euromoney* (1988, pp. 25-26) noted that "the biggest shock for the market was John Reed's May announcement of massive provisions, a move followed by other big money center banks. . . . 'The secondary debt market died almost overnight,' said one market participant."

acceleration of the growth of the banks' economic capacity to bear loss will facilitate the resumption of spontaneous lending. This will benefit the countries that have continued to service their debt and those troubled countries that somehow manage to rehabilitate their creditworthiness. But the reduction in the supply of bailout loans may slow the rehabilitation process.

References

Bailey, Jeff, "Continental Illinois Ex-Chief Aids FDIC, Strategy Reversal Exemplifies Quirky Trial," *Wall Street Journal* (Apr. 1, 1987), p. 6.

Bank of England, "Country Debt Provisions," London, August 1987.

Bank for International Settlements (BIS), "Proposals for International Convergence of Capital Measurement and Capital Standards," Consultative Paper of the Committee on Banking Regulations and Supervisory Practices, Basle, December 1987.

Bartlett, Sarah, with William Glasgall, Blanca Riemer, and John Templeman, "A Stunner from the Citi," *Business Week* (June 1, 1987), pp. 42-43.

Beebe, Jack, "Bank Stock Performance since the 1970's," *Economic Review*, Federal Reserve Bank of San Francisco (Winter 1985), pp. 5-18.

Buser, Stephen A., Andrew Chen, and Edward J. Kane, "Federal Deposit Insurance Regulatory Policy and Optimal Bank Capital," *Journal of Finance*, 36 (March 1981), pp. 51-60.

Citicorp, *Financial Review and Form 10Q, Third Quarter 1987*, New York, 1987.

———, *Citicorp 1987 Annual Report*, New York, 1988.

Country Exposure Lending Survey, Washington, Federal Financial Institutions Examination Council, various issues.

Denny, Richard S., "Form 8-K, Current Report, June 16, 1987, Bankers Trust Corporation," Washington, Securities and Exchange Commission, 1987.

Eaton, Jonathan, Mark Gersovitz, and Joseph E. Stiglitz, "The Pure Theory of Country Risk," *European Economic Review*, 30 (June 1986), pp. 481-513.

Euromoney, "Secondary Markets, Anomalous but Profitable," *Global Debt*, supplement to *Euromoney and Corporate Finance* (January 1988), pp. 25-27, 30-31.

Financial Times, "Secondary Market Reflects Boosted LDC Reserves," *International Banking Report*, 19 (Dec. 21, 1987), pp. 359-360.

Fleming, Stewart, "Banks 'May Face' Latin American Loan Write-Offs," *Financial Times*, Jan. 8, 1987, p. 1.

General Accounting Office (GAO), *International Banking, Supervision of Overseas Lending Is Inadequate*, GAO–SIAD-88-87, Washington, May 1988.

Guttentag, Jack M., and Richard J. Herring, *The Current Crisis in International Lending*, The Brookings Institution, Washington, 1985a.

———, "Funding Risk in the International Interbank Market," in Wilfred J. Ethier and Richard C. Marston, eds., *International Financial Markets and Capital Flows: A Symposium in Honor of Arthur I. Bloomfield*, Essays in International Finance No. 157, Princeton University, International Finance Section, 1985b, pp. 19-32.

————, "Commercial Bank Lending to Developing Countries: From Overlending to Underlending to Structural Reform," in G. Smith and J. Cuddington, eds., *International Borrowing and Lending: What Have We Learned from Theory and Practice?* Washington, World Bank, 1985c, pp. 129-150.

————, *Disaster Myopia in International Banking*, Essays in International Finance No. 164, Princeton University, International Finance Section,1986a.

————, "Disclosure Policy and International Banking," *Journal of Banking and Finance*, 10 (March 1986b), pp. 75-97.

————, "Financial Innovations to Stabilize Credit Flows to Developing Countries," *Studies in Banking and Finance*, Supplement on the International Debt Problem, 3 (1986c), pp. 263-304.

Hanley, Thomas, James Rosenberg, Carla D'Arista, and Elizabeth Krahmer, "Impaired Value Recognition of Developing Country Loans," *Bank Weekly*, Salomon Brothers, Inc., Apr. 21, 1987.

Hanley, Thomas H., John D. Leonard, Carla D'Arista, Dina I. Oddis, and Merrill H. Ross, *Domestic and International Bank Stock Investing: A Global Aproach*, New York, Salomon Brothers, Inc., 1988a.

————, *A Review of Bank Performance: 1988 Edition*, New York, Salomon Brothers, Inc., 1988b.

Herring, Richard J., "The Economics of Workout Lending," *Journal of Money, Credit and Banking*, 21 (February 1989), pp. 1-15.

Herring, Richard J., and Prashant Vankudre, "Growth Oportunities and Risk-Taking by Financial Intermediaries," *Journal of Finance*, 42 (July 1987), pp. 583-599.

Ingersoll, Bruce, and Jeff Bailey, "First Chicago to Restate Results, Settling SEC Charges of Insufficient Loss Reserves," *Wall Street Journal* (June 11,1987), p. 7.

Jones, Thomas E., "Form 8-K, Current Report, May 19, 1987, Citicorp," New York, Securities and Exchange Commission, 1987.

Keefe Equity Research, *Keefe Banking Industry Studies*, 20 (Aug. 13, 1987).

Kyle, Steven C., and Jeffrey D. Sachs, "Developing Country Debt and the Market Value of Large Commercial Banks," National Bureau of Economic Research Working Paper No. 1470, September 1984.

McDermott, James J., Jr., "LDC Loss Provisions: Once is Not Enough," *Keefe Nationwide Bankscan*, 22 (Dec. 1), 1987.

Musumeci, James, and Joseph Sinkey, Jr., "The International Debt Crisis and Bank Security Returns Surrounding Citicorp's Loan-Loss-Reserve Decision of May 19, 1987," mimeographed abstract of a paper presented at the Federal Reserve Bank of Chicago Conference on Bank Structure and Competition, May 13, 1988.

Sachs, Jeffrey, "LDC Debt in the 1980s: Risk and Reforms," in Paul Wachtel, ed., *Crises in the Economic and Financial Structure*, Lexington, Mass., Lexington Books, 1982, pp. 197-243.

Sachs, Jeffrey, and Harry Huizinga, "U.S. Commercial Banks and the Developing-Country Debt Crisis," *Brookings Papers on Economic Activity*, Vol. 2, 1987, pp. 555-601.

Schoder, Stewart, and Prashant Vankudre, "The Market for Bank Stocks and Banks' Disclosure of Cross-Border Exposure: The 1982 Mexican Debt Crisis," *Studies in Banking and Finance*, Supplement on the International Debt Problem, 3 (1986), pp. 179-207.

Smirlock, Michael, and Howard Kaufold, "Bank Foreign Lending, Mandatory Disclosure Rules, and the Reaction of Bank Stock Prices to the Mexican Debt Crisis," *Journal of Business*, 60 (July 1987), pp. 347-364.

Stiglitz, Joseph, and Andrew Weiss, "Incentive Effects of Terminations," *American Economic Review*, 73 (December 1983), pp. 912-927.

Tobin, James, "The Commercial Banking Firm: A Simple Model," *Scandinavian Journal of Economics*, 84 (No. 4, 1982), pp. 495-530.

Truell, Peter, "Citicorp's Reed Takes Firm Stance on Third-World Debt, Chairman Aims to Stem Commercial Banks' Trend toward Concessions," *Wall Street Journal* (Feb. 4, 1987), p. 6.

Watson, Maxwell, Donald Mathieson, Russell Kincaid, David Folkerts-Landau, Klaus Regling, and Caroline Atkinson, *International Capital Markets, Developments and Prospects*, IMF World Economic and Financial Surveys, Washington, January 1988.

APPENDIX

BAILOUT LOANS

The distinguishing characteristic of a bailout loan is that part of the expected return on the loan is the improved prospect that the borrower will repay its outstanding indebtedness to the lender (the increase in the expected value of the old loan if the bailout loan is made). A lender is faced with the need to make a bailout loan when the borrower's ability to service outstanding indebtedness has fallen into doubt.

Our model of bailout lending assumes throughout that only a single lender is involved and that this lender is risk neutral. (If several lenders are involved, the opportunity cost should be adjusted to reflect one lender's expectation that it can ride free on the bailout loans made by other lenders. See Herring, 1989, for a discussion of this aspect of the problem.) The implications of dropping these assumptions are discussed in the text. In addition, we make the following assumptions, which are progressively relaxed as we develop the model:

- The bank is not constrained by capital requirements.
- The bank's capacity to bear loss exceeds its outstanding claims against the borrower plus the bailout loan. (Thus, the bank will not fail if the bailout loan is not successful.)
- The bank is not penalized so long as its capital position is above zero.
- Accounting magnitudes that differ from market values are ignored by creditors, investors, tax authorities, and regulators, so that only market values matter to the bank.

The Basic Model

A bank that seeks to maximize the expected return to its shareholders will make a bailout loan only when the total expected return on the new loan (including the improved prospect of collecting the old loan) is at least equal to the opportunity cost of funds.[1] It is convenient to begin by assuming that

---

[1] For convenience, it is assumed that the outstanding claims would be entirely lost in the absence of a bailout loan and that the outcome of the bailout loan is either repayment of the entire outstanding balance, including the bailout loan, or loss of the bailout loan and the outstanding claims. Nonetheless, intermediate outcomes may be readily accommodated. Since lending decisions depend solely on the expected value of loan outcomes—the product of the outcome and the probability that it will be realized—they can easily be reinterpreted in terms of alternative outcome/probability pairs.

the opportunity cost of making the bailout loan is the risk-free rate.[2] From this condition, we can derive an explicit expression for the maximum bailout loan that the lender will be willing to advance.

Let L = the amount of the bailout loan
E = the lender's outstanding claims on the borrower including accrued interest
i = the risk-free interest rate
$r = 1 + i$
z = the spread above the risk-free rate on the bailout loan
$w = r + z$
p = the exogenously determined probability that $E + Lw$ will be repaid in full
$1 - p$ = the probability that no repayment will be made
k = the capital/asset ratio required by law or regulation
s = the expected return that investors demand on the bank's equity
K = the bank's capacity to bear loss.[3]

The largest bailout loan the bank will be willing to make equates the expected return from the loan with the opportunity cost of funds:[4]

$$p(E + Lw - L) - (1 - p)L = Li .\tag{A-1}$$

The first product on the left-hand side of the equation is the expected net return if the loan succeeds, and the second product is the expected net loss if the loan fails.[5] Solving this expression for L_M, the maximum bailout loan the bank would be willing to make, yields:

$$L_M = pE/(r - pw) ,\tag{A-2}$$

where $K \geqslant E + L$.

The denominator is positive because, by definition, the expected return on the bailout loan (pw disregarding E) is less than the risk-free return (r). The maximum bailout loan the bank will be willing to make is larger the

---

[2] In equation (A-3) below, we characterize the opportunity cost of the bailout loan as the return the bank could achieve by repaying its own cost of funds.

[3] This is equivalent to the value of shareholders' equity, valued for this purpose on the assumption that E is in good standing.

[4] Note that this is equivalent to the condition that the gross expected return from the loan equals the gross opportunity cost of funds: $p(E + Lw) = Lr$. Subtracting L from each side of this equation yields equation (A-1). We have chosen to emphasize net expected returns rather than gross returns because it is net rather than gross returns that influence behavior in the case where shareholders can shift part of the loss of L to third parties.

[5] An analytically trivial (but empirically relevant) case arises when the bailout loan is made to clear up interest-rate arrearages. Since the bailout loan is *not* at risk, equation (A-1) becomes $pE + Lw = Li$, where Lw is now the amount of interest arrearage. Other things equal, the bank would be willing to make a loan equal to Lw even if p were negligible.

higher the exogenously determined probability of success and the higher the promised return on the new loan. An increase in the general level of interest rates will diminish the maximum amount the bank is willing to lend.[6] Finally, the larger the bank's outstanding exposure to the borrower, the larger the maximum bailout loan it will be willing to make.

We have treated p, the probability that the bailout loan will succeed, as exogenous, even though in a more general model p would depend on the size of the bailout loan (as well as on a host of other factors, such as macroeconomic conditions beyond the control of both the bank and the borrower). Bailout loans of different sizes would carry different probabilities of success. We assume that the particular value of p that enters equation (A-2) is the value associated with L^*, the loan size yielding the maximum probability of success, which depends on a number of factors exogenous to the model. A bank's lending decision will depend on L_M relative to L^*. If $L_M > L^*$, the bank will lend L^*, because that will yield the highest expected profit. If $L^* > L_M$, the bank will not make any bailout loan: if it is unprofitable to make a loan large enough to maximize the probability of success, it will also be unprofitable to make a smaller loan. For example, if L_M calculated from equation (A-2) is \$4.54 and $L^* > \$4.54$, the bank will not make a bailout loan.[7] If $L^* = \$4.54$, the bank will lend \$4.54, and if $L^* = \$3.0$, the bank will lend \$3.0.

When Capital Requirements Are Binding

If the bank is subject to binding capital requirements, equation (A-2) must be amended to reflect the cost of the additional capital necessary to support the bailout loan.[8] It is reasonable to assume that a binding capital requirement will raise the opportunity cost of making the loan, because shareholders, who hold the residual claim on the bank's earnings, will always

---

[6] This is true even though the bailout loan is priced at a margin above the risk-free rate. Note that equation (A-1) can be rewritten as

$$p[E + L(1 + i + z) - L] - (1 - p)L = Li .$$

An increase in i raises the cost of funds by Li, but it increases the expected return by pLi. So long as $p < 1$, that is, so long as there is some anticipated probability of default, an increase in i will raise the cost of funds more than it raises the expected return on the bailout loan. As a consequence, the maximum bailout loan the bank will be willing to make declines. This can also be inferred directly from equation (A-2), where the partial derivative of L_M with respect to i is negative.

[7] For this illustration, the following parameter values were assumed:

$$p = 0.5, r = 1.1, w = 1.1, E = 5, K = 20.$$

[8] We are grateful to Donald Mathieson and David Folkerts-Landau for suggesting that we analyze this case.

demand a higher return than depositors, who have a prior claim. (The Miller-Modigliani theorem does not apply to banks, because implicit or explicit government guarantees make it unnecessary for creditors to charge the bank a higher risk premium when equity declines).

Denoting the required capital/asset ratio as k and the rate of return on the bank's equity as s, the cost of funds for the bailout loan is $Li(1 - k) + Lsk$. Substituting this expression for the opportunity cost of funds in equation (A-1) yields a new expression for the maximum bailout loan the bank would be willing to make:

$$L_M = pE/[r - pw + k(s - i)] , \qquad \text{(A-3)}$$

where $K \geqslant E + L$. Since $s > i$, an increase in the required capital/asset ratio will reduce the maximum bailout loan.

We have derived this result as if the capital/asset ratio were generally applicable to all assets, in accordance with current U.S. regulations, but the result applies equally to cases where k is set with regard to the bailout loan. For example, a risk-weighted capital requirement establishes a particular k for the bailout loan. Mandatory provisions will have a similar impact. Thus increases in the risk weighting or in mandatory provisioning will reduce the willingness to make a bailout loan. General provisioning that raises the bank's capital above the required level relaxes the capital constraint, so that equation (A-2) becomes the relevant equation and the willingness to lend increases.

When the Bank Is Overexposed

When the bank's total exposure to the borrower exceeds the shareholders' equity position in the bank, the bank is overexposed and may be willing to extend a much larger loan than the previous analysis would imply. (For ease of exposition, we shall resume the assumption that capital requirements are not binding.) Since shareholders cannot lose more than their capital position in the bank, their computation of net expected returns must be amended to reflect the truncation of expected losses when the bank's total exposure to the borrower, $E + L$, rises above the shareholders' capital position, K:

$$p(E + Lw - L) - (1 - p) \min(L, K - E) = Li \qquad \text{(A-4)}$$

Just as before, the maximum bailout loan the bank is willing to advance equates the expected net return with the opportunity cost of the loan. In this more general statement of the expected return to shareholders, the expected loss increases with the size of the loan until the point at which the loan equals the part of the bank's capital position that is not exposed to the borrower. Beyond that point, the expected loss to the shareholders remains the same, since there is no more capital to be lost, even though the size of the loan increases. As a result, expected profits decline more slowly as the bailout

44

loan (plus the outstanding claims on the borrower) exceeds the bank's capital position.

Figure A-1 illustrates this point for two banks that have identical exposures to the borrower but different capital positions. For Bank B exposure to the borrower is 50 percent of capital, while for Bank C exposure is 75 percent of capital.[9] Bank C can shift losses to third parties when the loan size exceeds $5 billion, but Bank B cannot shift losses until the loan exceeds $10 billion. Consequently, Bank C will be willing to make a substantially larger bailout loan than Bank B. Moreover, for any given loan size, Bank C perceives at least as high a net expected return as Bank B.

FIGURE A-1
SIZE OF MAXIMUM BAILOUT LOAN

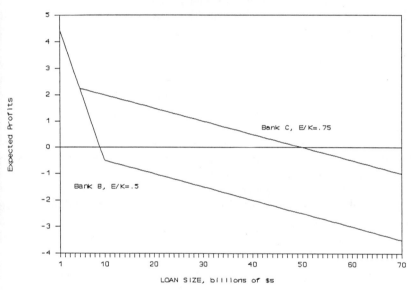

The very large exposure relative to capital of several major banks raises the possibility that some banks may have made decisions on the basis of the segment of the expected-profits function that applies when $K - E < L$.[10] For this segment, the maximum acceptable bailout loan is

$$L_M = [E - K(1 - p)]/[i - p(i + z)], \tag{A-5}$$

where $K < E + L$.

[9] For this illustration, the following parameter values were assumed: $p = 0.5$, $r = 1.1$, $i = 0.1$, $w = 1.1$, $E = 10$, $K = 20$ for Bank B, and $K = 15$ for Bank C.

[10] It should be noted that the exposure relevant to such an assessment should include claims on all borrowers whose repayment prospects would be adversely affected if the bailout loan is not extended.

Just as in equation (A-3), the bank will be willing to make a larger loan the higher the probability that the bailout loan will succeed, the lower the level of interest rates, and the larger the bank's exposure to the borrower. What is strikingly different, however, is that in this case the bank's capital position directly affects the bank's willingness to lend. The lower the bank's capital position, the larger the maximum acceptable bailout loan.

When the Capital Shortfall Is Subject to Penalty

A bank may be subject to a penalty if its capital position falls below some specific level, K^*.[11] We shall assume the penalty is smaller than the cost of increasing the bank's capital; otherwise, the bank would increase its capital rather than incur the penalty and the previous capital-constrained case applies. It is convenient to express the penalty as an explicit percentage charge, t, against the capital shortfall, $t(K^* - K)$, even though in practice it may take a variety of forms, such as constraints on expansion, restrictions on dividend payments, and so on.

The penalty will have an impact on the decision to make a bailout loan only if exposure to the borrower is large enough for the failure of the bailout loan to cause a shortfall from the bank's specified level of capital, K^*. For $K \geq K^* + L + E$, the bank will not have to pay the penalty even if the bailout loan fails, the penalty is irrelevant, and equation (A-2) describes the maximum bailout loan. The penalty will matter, however, when K falls below this amount. Precisely how it matters depends on whether the bank will be subject to a penalty even if the bailout loan is not made.

Consider the first case, where $K^* + L + E \geq K \geq K^* + E$, in which the bank's capital will fall below K^* if the bailout loan fails but will remain above K^* if the bailout loan is not made. In this instance, the expected return from the bailout loan must be revised to include the cost of the penalty that will be incurred if the bailout loan fails:

$$p(E + Lw - L) - (1 - p)\{L + t[K^* - (K - L - E)]\} \geq Li, \qquad \text{(A-6)}$$

for $K^* + E + L > K \geq K^* + E$.

The maximum bailout loan the bank will be willing to advance is

$$L_M = \{Ep - (1 - p)t[K^* - (K - E)]\}/[r - pw + (1 - p)t],$$

for $K^* + E + L > K \geq K^* + E$.

The partial derivative of equation (A-7) with respect to K is positive, so that as K rises from $K = K^* + E$ to $K = K^* + E + L$ an increase in K will increase the bank's willingness to make a bailout loan. In effect, the size of the potential penalty decreases as K increases, and it has a smaller and smaller impact on the decision to make a bailout loan.

[11] We are grateful to Andrew Crockett for suggesting that we analyze this case.

The impact of an increase in capital on the willingness to lend differs, however, when K falls within the range

$$K^* + E > K \geq L + E + t[K^* - (K - E - L)] \text{ and } K - E - L > 0 .$$

When the bank's capital is within this range, the bank will be obliged to pay a penalty if the bailout loan is not made (and E is consequently charged off) and also if the bailout loan is made and fails (so that both E and L must be charged off). Moreover, since $K \geq L + E + t[K^* - (K - E - L)]$, the entire loss including the penalty is borne by the shareholders. In this case, the expected return must be adjusted to reflect both the cost if the bailout loan is made and fails and the cost if the bailout loan is not made:

$$p(E + Lw - L) - (1 - p)[L + t(K^* - (K - L - E))]$$
$$\geq Li - t[K^* - (K - E)] , \tag{A-8}$$

where $K^* + E > K \geq L + E + t[K^* - (K - E - L)]$ and $K - E - L > 0$. This implies that the maximum bailout loan that the bank would be willing to make is:

$$L_M \{Ep + pt[K^* - (K - E)]\}/[r - pw + (1 - p)t] , \tag{A-9}$$

where $K^* + E > K \geq L + E + t[K^* - (K - E - L)]$ and $K - E - L > 0$.

The partial derivative of equation (A-9) with respect to K is negative. In contrast to the previous case, an increase in capital within this range will reduce the willingness to lend because the penalty that must be paid if the bailout loan is not made declines as K rises. This response is even stronger if the bank's capital falls within the range

$$L + E + t[K^* - \max(K - E - L, 0)] > K \geq E + t[K^* - (K - E)] .$$

In this case, the bank's shareholders will pay a penalty if the bailout loan is not made and E is charged off, but since K is not large enough to cover the loss of L and the penalty on the additional shortfall, the shareholders will not pay the full penalty if the bailout loan fails. Thus, on balance, the penalty provides an incentive to make the bailout loan.

If the bank's capital is less than E, the penalty is irrelevant. Since the bank's capital would be depleted if E were charged off, the penalty does not influence the lending decision; under circumstances in which the bank would be obliged to pay, it would be unable to pay. Hence, equation (A-5) describes the bank's behavior and, just as in equation (A-5), capital increases reduce the willingness to lend.

When Book Values Matter

When bank managers perceive a cost in *reporting* a decline in the market value of an asset, so that book values matter, the incentive to make a bailout loan will be enhanced. By making a bailout loan, the bank not only has a chance of retrieving the outstanding loans but also, by enabling the borrower to stay current on interest payments, the bank can delay—perhaps indefinitely—charging off its outstanding exposure.

The preceding analysis can be extended to this more complicated case by adjusting the opportunity cost of making the bailout loan to reflect the perceived cost of charging off the outstanding exposure if the risk-free investment is chosen and the bailout loan is *not* made. The perceived cost of charging off a loan can be expressed as the product of q times the book value of the bank's claims on the borrower. The loss in the event that the bailout loan fails must also be increased to reflect the perceived cost of charging off both the outstanding exposure and the bailout loan.

If losses are fully borne by shareholders, the expected return to the bailout loan, and the opportunity cost with which it is equated, become:

$$p(E + Lw - L) - (1 - p)[L + q(E + L)] = Li - qE , \qquad (A\text{-}10)$$

where $K \geqslant L + E$.

This condition implies that the maximum loan the bank will be willing to undertake is

$$L_M = [pE(1 + q)] / [r - pw + q(1 + p)], \qquad (A\text{-}11)$$

where $K \geqslant L + E$.

The higher the perceived cost in accepting a charge-off, the larger the maximum bailout loan.[12] As before, the fact that the loss to shareholders cannot exceed their capital position implies that there is a kink in the expected profit function at loan size $K < L + E$. The general expression for the expected return to shareholders is thus

$$p(E + Lw - L) - (1 - p)\min[K - E, L + q(L + E)]$$
$$= Li - qE . \qquad (A\text{-}12)$$

In the case where the bank is overexposed, so that $K < L + E$, the maximum bailout loan is

$$L_M = [E(1 + q) - K(1 - p)]/[i - p(z + i)] , \qquad (A\text{-}13)$$

where $K < L + E$.

Equation (A-13) is the same as equation (A-5), except that the return on the bailout loan is higher for any given set of values of the other variables.

---

[12] As a first approximation, the cost is likely to be a decreasing function of the gap between the book value of the bank's capital position K, and the capital position that regulators or creditors deem prudent, K^*, so that $q = q(K - K^*)$ and $q' < 0$.

And, as before, the willingness to make a bailout loan declines as K increases until $K = E + L$, at which point further increases in K have no effect. If q is a declining function of K, which is reasonable, the decline would be more rapid than that implied by equation (A-5), since the greater the bank's ability to absorb losses, the smaller the advantage in avoiding a charge-off.

PUBLICATIONS OF THE
INTERNATIONAL FINANCE SECTION

Notice to Contributors

The International Finance Section publishes at irregular intervals papers in four series: ESSAYS IN INTERNATIONAL FINANCE, PRINCETON STUDIES IN INTERNATIONAL FINANCE, SPECIAL PAPERS IN INTERNATIONAL ECONOMICS, and REPRINTS IN INTERNATIONAL FINANCE. ESSAYS and STUDIES are confined to subjects in international finance. SPECIAL PAPERS are surveys of the literature suitable for courses in colleges and universities.

An ESSAY should be a lucid exposition of a theme, accessible not only to the professional economist but to other interested readers. It should therefore avoid technical terms, should eschew mathematics and statistical tables (except when essential for an understanding of the text), and should rarely have footnotes.

A STUDY or SPECIAL PAPER may be more technical. It may include statistics and algebra and may have many footnotes. STUDIES and SPECIAL PAPERS may also be longer than ESSAYS; indeed, these two series are meant to accommodate manuscripts too long for journal articles and too short for books.

To facilitate prompt evaluation, please submit three copies of your manuscript. Retain one for your files. The manuscript should be typed on one side of 8½ by 11 strong white paper. All material should be double-spaced—text, excerpts, footnotes, tables, references, and figure legends. For more complete guidance, prospective contributors should send for the Section's style guide before preparing their manuscripts.

How to Obtain Publications

A mailing list is maintained for free distribution of all new publications to college, university, and public libraries and nongovernmental, nonprofit research institutions.

Individuals and organizations not qualifying for free distribution can receive all publications—ESSAYS, STUDIES, SPECIAL PAPERS, and REPRINTS—by paying a fee of $30 (inside and outside U.S.) to cover the period January 1 through December 31.

ESSAYS and REPRINTS can also be ordered from the Section at $4.50 per copy, and STUDIES and SPECIAL PAPERS at $6.50. Payment MUST be included with the order and MUST be made in U.S. dollars. PLEASE INCLUDE $1.25 FOR POSTAGE AND HANDLING. (These charges are waived on orders from persons or organizations in countries whose foreign-exchange regulations prohibit such remittances.) For airmail delivery outside U.S., Canada, and Mexico, there is an additional charge of $1.50.

All manuscripts, correspondence, and orders should be addressed to:

International Finance Section
Department of Economics, Dickinson Hall
Princeton University
Princeton, New Jersey 08544-1017

Subscribers should notify the Section promptly of a change of address, giving the old address as well as the new one.

51

List of Recent Publications

To obtain a complete list of publications, write the International Finance Section.

ESSAYS IN INTERNATIONAL FINANCE

147. Edmar Lisboa Bacha and Carlos F. Díaz Alejandro, *International Financial Intermediation: A Long and Tropical View*. (May 1982)
148. Alan A. Rabin and Leland B. Yeager, *Monetary Approaches to the Balance of Payments and Exchange Rates*. (Nov. 1982)
149. C. Fred Bergsten, Rudiger Dornbusch, Jacob A. Frenkel, Steven W. Kohlhagen, Luigi Spaventa, and Thomas D. Willett, *From Rambouillet to Versailles: A Symposium*. (Dec. 1982)
150. Robert E. Baldwin, *The Inefficacy of Trade Policy*. (Dec. 1982)
151. Jack Guttentag and Richard Herring, *The Lender-of-Last Resort Function in an International Context*. (May 1983)
152. G. K. Helleiner, *The IMF and Africa in the 1980s*. (July 1983)
153. Rachel McCulloch, *Unexpected Real Consequences of Floating Exchange Rates*. (Aug. 1983)
154. Robert M. Dunn, Jr., *The Many Disappointments of Floating Exchange Rates*. (Dec. 1983)
155. Stephen Marris, *Managing the World Economy: Will We Ever Learn?* (Oct. 1984)
156. Sebastian Edwards, *The Order of Liberalization of the External Sector in Developing Countries*. (Dec. 1984)
157. Wilfred J. Ethier and Richard C. Marston, eds., with Kindleberger, Guttentag and Herring, Wallich, Henderson, and Hinshaw, *International Financial Markets and Capital Movements: A Symposium in Honor of Arthur I. Bloomfield*. (Sept. 1985)
158. Charles E. Dumas, *The Effects of Government Deficits: A Comparative Analysis of Crowding Out*. (Oct. 1985)
159. Jeffrey A. Frankel, *Six Possible Meanings of "Overvaluation": The 1981-85 Dollar*. (Dec. 1985)
160. Stanley W. Black, *Learning from Adversity: Policy Responses to Two Oil Shocks*. (Dec. 1985)
161. Alexis Rieffel, *The Role of the Paris Club in Managing Debt Problems*. (Dec. 1985)
162. Stephen E. Haynes, Michael M. Hutchison, and Raymond F. Mikesell, *Japanese Financial Policies and the U.S. Trade Deficit*. (April 1986)
163. Arminio Fraga, *German Reparations and Brazilian Debt: A Comparative Study*. (July 1986)
164. Jack M. Guttentag and Richard J. Herring, *Disaster Myopia in International Banking*. (Sept. 1986)
165. Rudiger Dornbusch, *Inflation, Exchange Rates, and Stabilization*. (Oct. 1986)
166. John Spraos, *IMF Conditionality: Ineffectual, Inefficient, Mistargeted*. (Dec. 1986)
167. Rainer Stefano Masera, *An Increasing Role for the ECU: A Character in Search of a Script*. (June 1987)
168. Paul Mosley, *Conditionality as Bargaining Process: Structural-Adjustment Lending, 1980-86*. (Oct. 1987)

169. Paul A. Volcker, Ralph C. Bryant, Leonhard Gleske, Gottfried Haberler, Alexandre Lamfalussy, Shijuro Ogata, Jesús Silva-Herzog, Ross M. Starr, James Tobin, and Robert Triffin, *International Monetary Cooperation: Essays in Honor of Henry C. Wallich*. (Dec. 1987)
170. Shafiqul Islam, *The Dollar and the Policy-Performance-Confidence Mix*. (July 1988)
171. James Boughton, *The Monetary Approach to Exchange Rates: What Now Remains?* (Oct. 1988)
172. Jack M. Guttentag and Richard Herring, *Accounting for Losses on Sovereign Debt: Implications for New Lending*. (May 1989)

PRINCETON STUDIES IN INTERNATIONAL FINANCE

49. Peter Bernholz, *Flexible Exchange Rates in Historical Perspective*. (July 1982)
50. Victor Argy, *Exchange-Rate Management in Theory and Practice*. (Oct. 1982)
51. Paul Wonnacott, *U.S. Intervention in the Exchange Market for DM, 1977-80*. (Dec. 1982)
52. Irving B. Kravis and Robert E. Lipsey, *Toward an Explanation of National Price Levels*. (Nov. 1983)
53. Avraham Ben-Bassat, *Reserve-Currency Diversification and the Substitution Account*. (March 1984)
*54. Jeffrey Sachs, *Theoretical Issues in International Borrowing*. (July 1984)
55. Marsha R. Shelburn, *Rules for Regulating Intervention under a Managed Float*. (Dec. 1984)
56. Paul De Grauwe, Marc Janssens, and Hilde Leliaert, *Real-Exchange-Rate Variability from 1920 to 1926 and 1973 to 1982*. (Sept. 1985)
57. Stephen S. Golub, *The Current-Account Balance and the Dollar: 1977-78 and 1983-84*. (Oct. 1986)
58. John T. Cuddington, *Capital Flight: Estimates, Issues, and Explanations*. (Dec. 1986)
59. Vincent P. Crawford, *International Lending, Long-Term Credit Relationships, and Dynamic Contract Theory*. (March 1987)
60. Thorvaldur Gylfason, *Credit Policy and Economic Activity in Developing Countries with IMF Stabilization Programs*. (Aug. 1987)
61. Stephen A. Schuker, *American "Reparations" to Germany, 1919-33: Implications for the Third-World Debt Crisis*. (July 1988)
62. Steven B. Kamin, *Devaluation, External Balance, and Macroeconomic Performance: A Look at the Numbers*. (Aug. 1988)
63. Jacob A. Frenkel and Assaf Razin, *Spending, Taxes, and Deficits: International-Intertemporal Approach*. (Dec. 1988)
64. Jeffrey A. Frankel, *Obstacles to International Macroeconomic Policy Coordination*. (Dec. 1988)

SPECIAL PAPERS IN INTERNATIONAL ECONOMICS

13. Louka T. Katseli-Papaefstratiou, *The Reemergence of the Purchasing Power Parity Doctrine in the 1970s*. (Dec. 1979)
*14. Morris Goldstein, *Have Flexible Exchange Rates Handicapped Macroeconomic Policy?* (June 1980)
15. Gene M. Grossman and J. David Richardson, *Strategic Trade Policy: A Survey of Issues and Early Analysis*. (April 1985)

REPRINTS IN INTERNATIONAL FINANCE

22. Jorge Braga de Macedo, *Exchange Rate Behavior with Currency Inconvertibility*. [Reprinted from *Journal of International Economics*, 12 (Feb. 1982).] (Sept. 1982)
23. Peter B. Kenen, *Use of the SDR to Supplement or Substitute for Other Means of Finance*. [Reprinted from George M. von Furstenberg, ed., *International Money and Credit: The Policy Roles*, Washington, IMF, 1983, Chap. 7.] (Dec. 1983)
24. Peter B. Kenen, *Forward Rates, Interest Rates, and Expectations under Alternative Exchange Rate Regimes*. [Reprinted from *Economic Record*, 61 (Sept. 1985).] (June 1986)
25. Jorge Braga de Macedo, *Trade and Financial Interdependence under Flexible Exchange Rates: The Pacific Area*. [Reprinted from Augustine H.H. Tan and Basant Kapur, eds., *Pacific Growth and Financial Interdependence*, Sydney, Australia, Allen and Unwin, 1986, Chap. 13.] (June 1986)

54

NOTICE

In our previous mailing, you received Study No. 63 by Jacob A. Frenkel and Assaf Razin entitled *Spending, Taxes, and Deficits: International-Intertemporal Approach*. The inside front cover refers, by mistake, to "Jeffrey A. Frenkel" as the co-author of the Study. It should, of course, be Jacob A. Frenkel. Our apologies.

ISBN 0-88165-079-